CARIBBEAN IMMIGRANTS: A SOCIO-DEMOGRAPHIC PROFILE

Wolseley W. Anderson

Canadian Scholars' Press Inc.   Toronto   1993

Caribbean Immigrants: A Socio-Demographic Profile

First published in 1993 by
Canadian Scholars' Press Inc.
180 Bloor St. W., Ste. 402
Toronto, Ontario
M5S 2V6

Canadian Cataloguing in Publication Data

Main entry under title:

Caribbean Immigrants: A Socio-Demographic Profile

Includes bibliographical references.
ISBN 1-55130-013-3

Printed and bound in Canada

Acknowledgement

This book was assisted financially with a generous grant
from Multiculturalism and Citizenship Canada,
Department of the Secretary of State.

Page layout by Brad Horning, Toronto.

TABLE OF CONTENTS

LIST OF TABLES

LIST OF FIGURES

ACKNOWLEDGEMENTS

The idea of a monograph on the Caribbean-Canadians was sown and nurtured in a third year Social Science course entitled "The Caribbean Experience in Multicultural Canada," in which the author has been engaged as course director for well over a decade. In that pedagogic environment, teacher and students, over the years, critically examined the theory and practice of arrival and integration into multicultural Canadian society. It was seen that there was a need for preparing and recording a data base pertinent to immigration and the integration of immigrants on their arrival.

It is therefore to my students of Social Science 3270.06A over the years that thanks must go in the first place. They have been essential to initiating, sustaining and focussing the dialogue.

Expressions of thanks are due also to my West Indian colleagues with whom the project has been exhaustingly and sometimes bitterly discussed along the way. In particular, mention must be made of Professors Rudy Grant and George Eaton, who read and commented on the manuscript at different stages.

But, without the goading of my publisher and the funding to complete the project, the Caribbean-Canadians would not now be taking a place on your shelf. Thank you, Jack Wayne. You were a key person in both areas. Thanks, too, to the Document Processing Unit at York and its very helpful team of workers who exercised infinite patience with my idiosyncrasies. Throughout the exercise, it was the computer expertise of Al Rodwell-Simon, my good friend, that, like a beacon, lighted the field ahead. Thank you, Al.

Finally, grateful acknowledgement must be expressed to the Writing and Publications Program of the Secretary of State Department, Multiculturalism, for making available a grant to assist in the publication of this book, which I hope will provide a welcome contribution to inter-cultural understanding in Canada.

W.W.A.

INTRODUCTION

For reasons that are as complex as the human mind can fathom, it has been an inconclusive and an unsettling task to set up meaningful boundaries, in theory and in practice, between the rubric Black and that sub-set of the Black experience which is Caribbean or West Indian in essence. Inconclusive, perhaps, because we just have not worked hard enough yet in separating rhetoric from praxis. Unsettling, maybe, in as much as the absence of a carefully defined sense of identity in a complex mass society such as today's can be seen to promise escalating measures of adjustment difficulties for the group and the individual. From a Caribbean-Canadian perspective, it is most inconclusive and most unsettling for the West Indian youth in particular. And yet, among those who share, or would share, a common sense of belonging, the skill of being able to sharpen distinctions without repudiating common cause provides the penetrative edge of ethno-cultural group action in a multi-ethnic setting. Caribbean reality flows from a "fibrous," not a "tap," root system.

The central purpose of this monograph is to make a contribution towards promoting, in both the private and the public domain, a higher level of conscious understanding of the Caribbean ethno-cultural group and its presence in Canada. It attempts to do this while holding a careful balance between self-definition and the view of self as seen by others—the subjective and objective views of identity. In this way, the monograph adopts two complementary approaches. One explores socio-historical context, and the other provides socio-demographic materials and insights. It is hoped that in the interplay of these two approaches a more penetrating understanding of the challenge to Caribbean-Canadians of integrating into Canada, and a demonstration of the collective strength and will to do so confidently and progressively, will have been stimulated.

It is a deftly woven fabric of inter-cultural mix which gives the Caribbean—the West Indies—its own unique character. As such, it reflects an exciting variant which enriches the African diaspora. At the same time, inherent in the compound or mixture (and indeed it has been both) are the cultural contributions from the indigenous Amerindians, from Europe, Asia south and east, and elsewhere—contributions which, in equal measure, enrich the geo-cultural diaspora from which they sprang. Thus, the Caribbean must be presented and understood as an entity in its own multicultural right, without this being construed as divisive to the Black cause—or the Asian or the European cause for that matter. The sub-sets that fall within Caribbean multicultural Canada usually "do not detract from wider loyalties to community and country."[1] This is the very logic in which democratic society is grounded.

Based on immigrant inflows in the post-World War II period alone, the number of West Indians arriving in Canada is in the vicinity of 350,000. The racial and linguistic plurality of these people, the national ideological and constitutional systems, the national political and administrative regimes under which they have lived prior to arrival in Canada, all constitute a complexity that is rivalled in the Western world perhaps only by Canada itself. Yet, there is a distinct identity that they would often assert about themselves. And, equally so, there will be voices which question the existence of any such common identity and the basis on which it is premised. All of this describes a certain vibrancy, a dynamism about the society which challenges the imagination and stimulates the desire for further study.

The monograph is in two parts. In the first part an examination is made of the larger historical context in which Caribbean reality has emerged. The first section of Part 1 deals with the West Indian story in the metaphoric sense of a 'cultural inflorescence.' One of the themes dealt with is the similarity in historical experience shared between the Caribbean and Canada. This section also suggests the hypothesis that race, not similarity of historical background, has determined the status of West Indians on arrival and after arriving in Canada. Third, this section posits that creolization in the Caribbean has been a process not dissimilar to the one which has led to the development of multiculturalism in Canada. Part 1, additionally, attempts to briefly analyse some of the broader economic and socio-political factors whose historical persistence has dominated the pattern of relationship between Britain and her colonies in the first place and, as a result, between Canada and the Caribbean. Then, in a very brief chapter, the constituent territories of the people referred to throughout the monograph as the Caribbean-Canadians are listed.

After examining some of the major signposts of Canadian immigration policy since the post-World War II years, Part 1 proceeds to suggest that contemporary 'push-pull' factors in Caribbean-Canadian immigration are essentially part of historical and commercial relations between the two entities. It posits that all that may be new since the 1960s is the replacing of sugar by human resources as the principal commodity of Caribbean export to Canada.

From this background, Part 2 presents the socio-demographic profile of Caribbean immigrants to Canada in the quarter of a century between 1966 and 1990. In a number of sections it examines the volume of this immigration and the percentage of total Canadian immigration it has constituted over the years. The major Caribbean sources (countries) from which the annual inflows come and the provinces to which they intend to go are presented. Age and gender characteristics are examined and the implications for public policy as well as for ethno-specific action discussed. In particular, this discussion raises issues associated with daycare and schooling, issues of welfare for the elderly, and the question of youth services. A penultimate chapter of Part 2 is devoted to an examination of intended workforce participation by Caribbean newcomers. The categories of skills (and level of education) they bring with them are examined both internally and comparatively; and again, the discussion raises issues such as the efficient use of these resources by employers in both the public and the private sectors. The final chapter of the monograph presents a brief summary of socio-demographic findings and a concluding discussion which draws attention to the troubling issues of immigration and integration generally and the challenges that face Caribbean-Canadians as they seek to negotiate their way into the many institutional structures of a country in which a fierce race relations battle rages.

As its concluding thought, the monograph argues that the integration process is an essential complement of any successful immigration policy. For the Caribbean-Canadians, a progressive integration process is a function of both self-help and the development of effective partnerships between the newcoming community and the institutions and structures of the host society.

There is growing evidence that the structures of the socio-cultural duality that was Canada are under increasing scrutiny and pressure to change to accommodate a new socio-cultural plurality. Critical institutions such as the law, schooling and the workplace, conventionally have, and will continue to resist change. Hierarchical host societies stratified by race, ethnicity or whatever other distinguishing criteria must be expected to reveal diverse forms of racist attitudes and practices of discrimination. It is the inescapable task of all newcomers to galvanise their will and resources in order to effect meaningful and satisfying changes for integration into these institutions. Caribbean-Canadians should expect it to be no different in their Canadian experience.

ENDNOTES

1. Pierre E. Trudeau, "Federal Government's Response to Book IV of the Report of the Royal Commission on Bilingualism and Biculturalism." Ministry of Supply and Services, Ottawa, 1971.

PART 1

SOCIO-HISTORICAL BACKGROUND

CHAPTER 1

INFLORESCENCES AND MOSAICS:
CARIBBEAN-CANADIAN SIMILARITIES

Where the flaming poinceana
And the ever-waving palm,
And the low palmetto scrub
Are broadly cast,
O'er the sunny islands smiling
Still in tempest and in calm,
Lives the record of a strange
And storied past.[1]

From earliest times writers have seen the West Indian islands in the flowering, colourful image of the poem quoted above. Usually, the writers were referring particularly to the sunshine and flora of the Caribbean island, set "gem-like and fair," in a grand archipelago that hung from the tip of the Yucatan peninsula right across to the Guyana lowlands of South America. This sparkling chain separated the Atlantic from the more colourfully blue Caribbean: a chain of "little emerald islands with the sapphire sea between,"[2] where the waves of Atlantic Europe and the Amerindian/Caribbean met and mingled.

But the inflorescence that is the Caribbean today refers as well to the people of the region, arranged in clusters of colourful petals variegated by race, by religion, by language and dialect, and by ethnicity. The Caribbean faces and costumed bodies that appear on the covers of so many tourist brochures emphasize a characteristic Caribbean richness and a beauty which, when added to the Canadian picture, gives graphic meaning to the expression, "a mosaic within a colourful mosaic." How then has it come about—this mosaic within a mosaic—this Caribbean ethno-cultural section within a multicultural Canada? The rest of this chapter will be devoted to quickly telling that story.

Three principal themes will be sketched. The first one will suggest that, though their paths of development have been different, the historical circumstances which gave birth to Canada and to the Caribbean were similar. The second theme asserts that despite a shared historical experience within the British Commonwealth and Empire, the entry status of people from the Caribbean into Canada has been determined less by culture than by race. A third theme will observe that the creolization process in the Caribbean provided an experience not altogether dissimilar from Canadian cultural pluralism today. A brief elaboration on these themes will present a groundwork of implications and issues for later consideration.

The growing self-confidence of European nation states in the sixteenth, seventeenth and eighteenth centuries revealed itself in, among other things, the economic embrace by these states of the New World. The wealth, power and prestige that accrued from founding, maintaining and exploiting colonies was the foundation of European economic nationalism. The ideological principle was that colonies existed primarily for the enrichment of their respective mother countries through the primary commodities they produced and the markets they provided for metropolitan manufactured goods. This principle was effectively implemented through a network of tight navigation laws which directed the operations of both merchant and fighting navies. Thus, the mercantilist embrace of Europe at the same time enriched England, France, Spain and others while impoverishing their colonies such as Canada and the islands of the Caribbean. To eighteenth and nineteenth century imperial Britain both Canada and the Caribbean were colonies to be exploited. The somewhat spurious distinction between, *colonies de peuplement* and *colonies de l'exploitation* notwithstanding, the staple commodities of fur, fish and timber from Canada were not less important to metropolitan Britain than were the staples of sugar, rum and molasses from the Caribbean, even though sugar was king of all the staples.[3] Indeed, the mercantile interests of Britain at the time acted well to assure that there was inter-supportiveness between the staples from one part of the empire with those from another. The fish and the lumber required to meet the needs of the sugar cane plantations in the Caribbean were as important to the process of profit-making for the planter class as was the availability of rum to boost the morale of the 'fighting men' of the navies in the duties of trading with and defending all the colonies of the empire. Insofar as the metropolis was concerned, inter-supportiveness among the various parts of the hinterland, or the loci of production, was the hallmark of efficiency in, for and at the centre of decision-making.[4]

The nature of the staple had a very powerful influence on how the particular colonial society developed. In fact some staple theorists have argued that it is the interaction between the staple and the geographical terrain that determines the pattern of development in the early stages of the colony. Innis,[5] for example, has contended that fur, in Canada, linked the efforts of the trapper, the coureur-de-bois and the merchant across a variegated and challenging geographical terrain. At each one of these links in the chain private entrepreneurship could be and was stimulated. The conditions and possibility existed for small private enterprises or ventures gradually to arise in response to perceived needs in Canadian settlement communities. However, on the sugar cane plantations of the Caribbean, enclaved on the land as they were, entrepreneurship and private enterprise were inhibited, in fact prohibited, thereby accentuating a total authority structure, a rigid dependency syndrome. The plantation has been likened to Goffman's[6] model of a total institution. Beckford,[7] Goveia[8] and others have concurred, pointing out that the slaves who worked the cane fields and the sugar factories in gangs were not even considered human. They were property or chattel to be disposed of and otherwise exploited at the convenience and the bidding of the planter. The presence of millions of slaves for work on the plantations and relatively few white owners (a ratio that ranged from 10:1 in some places to as much as 30:1 in others)[9] made it necessary to devise harsh and cruel slave laws to keep the slaves disciplined, productive and submissive. But the slave laws did not only do that. In addition, they kept the white and black populations apart and at a social distance on the plantations. In this way, a caste system developed with whites at the top of the social pyramid, blacks at the bottom, and in the middle, a buffer group of mulattoes who were the offspring of black female slaves raped by white masters in exercise of their ruthless right of property. Upward or downward movement among these groups was virtually non-existent during the slavery period.[10]

It is to be noted that there was slavery in Canada as well.[11] Many of the Catholic seigneurs and the English nobility in the sixteenth century and after retained a retinue of slaves. But the phenomenon was not as widespread and deep-rooted as it was in the Caribbean. Remember, as we discussed above, that the nature of the staple and geography determine the economic and social forms and structures that emerge. In Canada there was no staple such as sugar that required a cheap reservoir of plentiful labour all year round. Therefore, there was no need for total institutions like the plantation system and slavery; consequently such forms did not develop.[12] There was always need for labour and, with many entrepreneurs in early Canada, a propensity to exploit labour. But the motivation to monopolize the human body and mind and to make them a part of property was not really there. The agonies and horrors of the Canadian lumber camps have been well documented, but the human degradation of plantation slavery was a phenomenon without parallel within the annals of human cruelty. Other consequences followed from this difference in type of colony.

The "settlement" emphasis in colonial Canada did not completely protect it from exploitation by the "mother country" which was, in the first place, its raison d'etre. But its activities of trapping, homesteading, fishing and lumbering provided adequate scope for the emergence of a limited domestic market situation. With the leadership of significant institutions such as the Church, the Hudson's Bay Company and the Royal Canadian Mounted Police the basis of a market economy and its supportive infrastructure and superstructure were being laid. Linkages of the sort that would provide spread effects for goods and services in the economy were allowed to develop. At the same time perceptible class differentiation between homesteaders and habitants, and between merchants and the nobility, could be seen to reveal greater articulation over time. Yet, fundamental to Canadian society and the pattern it would take was the conquest of the French by the English and the ensuing elements of distrust and separation that that would engender as a characteristic feature of social reality from 1763 on. Almost without respite since then, race, language, religion, and with them, class, have been major preoccupations of the body politic. And immigration policy has been forged as a convenient instrument in effecting and maintaining the required balance between those forces— economic, cultural and social—and overall population growth. But the "Two Nations" vision of Canada has always been myopic. The coming of the United Empire Loyalists after 1776, the arrival of batches of Maroons from Jamaica during and after the last decade of the eighteenth century, the operation of the Underground Railroad before and during the American Civil War—all these (not to mention the post-World War II arrivals) have increased the Black presence in Canadian society.[13] But blacks did not enjoy preferred status as Canadian immigrants. Nor did Asiatics. Large scale immigration from the Orient, or more specifically from the Asian Pacific Triangle, as it was called, was never encouraged, despite the labour needs of the CPR. But these immigrants' presence in the country could not be denied. When all this is coupled with the harsh measures of continuing internal colonialism meted out to the Native Peoples of Canada there can be little argument about two features of the society. One is that a form of cultural pluralism has existed in it for some considerable time. The other is that overt and systemic forms of racism have existed and continue to exist within it.

The Caribbean too, as it emerged as a colonial society, was not, as we shall see, devoid of its own form of cultural pluralism and deep-seated racism. The caste-like situation which existed during slavery began, after Emancipation in 1834, to give way to a system of class stratification based initially on race, but progressively becoming influenced in the later years of the century by factors such as wealth and education. Essentially, however, race, colour and class remained as divisive elements in the society.[14] In the economic domain, the planters after Emancipation still had to protect their interests in sugar, and sought for greater production and productivity to outweigh the shifting importance and declining price the commodity was fetching on the market. Even if sugar was now to be produced by wage rather than slave labour, in the minds of the planters the reservoir of cheap labour would still have to be maintained. Of course they turned to immigration for the answer. Nineteenth century immigration to the Caribbean included cosmopolitan thousands from Portugal and Madeira, China and Hong Kong, India and the Middle East—all superimposed on the freed African and the Amerindian population where, as in the case of Guyana, they still existed. The result of this stream of immigration on Caribbean societies, especially those with considerable land space like Guyana, Trinidad and Jamaica, was to provide the basis for a cultural inflorescence in which race, colour, language, religion, folkways and ethnicity all mixed and mingled beneath the influence of the sovereign values of the British colonizer.

What the above discussion has shown is that the colonial pasts of Canada and the Caribbean left them with some interesting similarities. Among these was the plural society phenomenon and the stratified nature of both societies. To take the observation even further, we will state that by the middle of the twentieth century both societies, plural in nature, were also stratified by race and ethnicity. In both cases the examination would reveal a picture in which anglo-celtic protestants are at the top of the social pyramid and Blacks and Native Peoples at the bottom. In terms of stratification, Porter's *Vertical Mosaic*[16] reveals a pattern for Canada in the late 1960s which is not that much different from Lowenthal's picture of *West Indian Societies*[15] in the early 1970s. Where the former identifies race and ethnicity as the class mobility factors, the latter sees them as race and colour. After independence in the Caribbean, however, the factors of education, wealth and political participation have combined to place many Afro-Caribbeans at the top of their respective societies. A most interesting and revealing piece of research might seek to ascertain how much of a reinforcing element to self-worth among young West Indians this might be in comparison with young African-Americans.

Thus, in looking at the significant waves of Caribbean immigrants that began coming into Canada in the 1960s, the investigator must take into account the fact that both presenting and host societies have shared a strong similarity of colonial background. Their origins lay in staple producing economies dominated by a mother country. Both societies have been built up by immigration. Both societies are pluralistic, differentiated by race, language, religion and ethnicity. They have both been influenced by the values and the social and political institutions of Britain. They were both socialized by the hidden agenda in British colonialism to "love the land that bore you but the Empire best of all."[17] Racism has been as endemic, systemic and pervasive in Canada as it has been in the Caribbean experience.

What, then, can these experiences both offer to the success of inter-cultural relations in contemporary Canada? A student from the Caribbean in emotional frustration, said: "Don't tell me about multicultural; I *am* multicultural; I have lived it. You are now coming to understand it, perhaps, thanks to Trudeau."[18] What did he really mean when he said he lived it? Perhaps we should spend a few moments looking at the process of creolization in the Caribbean and, in doing so, try to establish what sense of identity Caribbean people derived from it.

The Caribbean experience is, indeed, a unique one. For it is the one and only instance where all three races—negroid, mongoloid and caucasoid—and a number of civilizations representative of Western Europe, of West Africa, of Asian, Chinese and Syrian civilizations, of Amerindian cultures in all their tribal complexities, met in one place devoid of a common referent cultural context. Cortez and Pizarro had put the Amerindian to the sword just as Raleigh and de Berrio had sought in vain for the shining towers of Manoa and El Dorado.[19] Thus, slaughter by sword and frustration born of chimeras marked the birthing crucibles of Caribbean societies. In a quaint admixture of fact and myth, co-existence of inferiority and superiority complexes, amid the great paradoxes of salvation and domination, the genetic imperative of the dominant and the recessive yielded up its filial stock—the Caribbean 'thoroughbred' person.

The fabricated civilization of 'King Sugar' was premised on the superior power and values of the colonizer, holding in chains and at ransom the collective will of a people unable to participate proactively in the formation and evolution of their culture. There has been the strongest suggestion in many quarters, scholarly and otherwise, that the culture of the slave plantation was a culture of self-annihilation and abject dependence. It was an existence that was neither proactive nor assertive but docile and subjected to the whims and fancies of the colonizer.[20] But any such suggestion is devoid of the psychological and the socio-biological insights which instruct that slavery corrupted both the colonizer and the colonized while making the latter stronger; that docility was a device for survival; and that defiance was the informing spirit of Toussaint L'Ouverture, Cuffy and Akara, Paul Bogle, Damon and the many other leaders of the slave revolts and rebellions across the eighteenth and nineteenth centuries.

The African cultural presence, the Black presence, is very much a part of this Euro-Afric-Asian drama. But it is not the only part. The creolization experience of the slavery period provided a spectrum of personality types that ranges from "Uncle Tom" to "Kunta Kinte."[21] The post-emancipation years intensified the sophistication of a process which saw the cultural genes of the many ethnic immigrant cultures survive not only at the local levels, but slowly and progressively meet, mingle and reinforce one another in myriads of syncretic combinations and forms at the public and national levels. What has emerged from this "indigenization" process, as Nettleford[22] points out, is a biological and social orchestra in which the drums and rhythms of Africa provide the background against which the strings of Europe and the flutes and pipes of India and Asia interplay in rich harmonious melody. The patterns of syncretism, revisionism and cultural revitalism are to be noted not only in the expressive art forms such as music, drama, and Pitchy Patchy.[23] They are there, too, as Case (1985)[24] and Lewis (1983)[25] remind us, in the dynamic vibrancy of literary endeavour and social and political thought.

In this way then, the Caribbean experience, the creolization process, is a multicultural experience. Whether the patterns of enculturation have been assimilative to the dominant British cultural forms (Smith, 1965)[26] or whether the pattern was reticulated and based on factors such as colour, religion and education (Despres, 1967)[27] is, in the final analysis less important than the realization that out of the experience has come a people with a common ancestry but complex and varied identities. For example, an Indo-Guyanese may define himself differently from a Sino-Jamaican even though they have the same spontaneously rhythmic response to reggae. The Afro-Trinidadian with rural roots and upbringing may be as responsive to elements of shango or pocomania as a Haitian from the southern province. But this same Afro-Trinidadian could be miles away, in a social sense, from another Afro-Trinidadian living in the residential spread of Valsayn or Maraval.[28] The cultural legacy is a rich organic whole but the properties within that whole are differently put together and no one Caribbean person reflects them all. Thus varying identities and personality types are sustained in a complex cultural milieu. Just as regional identity is complicated by the historic manner in which insular parochialisms were fostered and maintained by the British, so are personal identities rendered multi-dimensional by the complex interplay of factors such as race and religion, colour and class, dialect and folklore, all of which have been zealously preserved by the hierarchic nature of Caribbean societies and a basic geographic limitation that reduces contact. Despite the pervasive use and inference of the unifying pseudonym 'Black,' Caribbean personality is both prismatic and protean. And there is great need for programs of inter-disciplinary studies to take us to the truth behind the Black misnomer.[29]

These are the people, Caribbeans or West Indians who, for a generation since the introduction of a systematic points system to regulate immigrant inflows, have supplied just under 10 percent per annum of Canada's immigrant population. With the exception of those from Haiti, who are French speaking, they are members of the British Commonwealth of Nations to which Canada belongs. Their ancestors, like Canada's, had fought and died, in honour and in pride, against the German/Italian Axis in the Second World War. Yet these immigrants enjoy a very low entry status into Canada, certainly lower than that enjoyed by post-war German-Canadians or Italian-Canadians.

In 1947, when overt racism characterized Canada's immigration policy, the then Prime Minister, Mackenzie King, boldly announced that Canadians reserved the right to decide who would be invited to live amongst them.[30] And it was his undisputed right to do so. But the fact was that Caribbeans were not among the preferred groups. Yet a scheme to provide household assistance for Canadian families on was agreed between Canada and several West Indian territories, all of which at the time, enjoyed Crown Colony Government status with Britain. By 1956, the first batch of domestic servants from the Caribbean arrived in Canada. Caribbean citizens were deemed not good enough, so it seemed, to answer Canada's general immigration requirements, but in that section of the labour market that employed domestic labour Canada condescended to permit contractual landed status to a few.

Though the Caribbean peoples, as we have seen earlier, are of many different territorial, racial and ethnic backgrounds they still are stereotyped by the Canadian host society as Blacks or Jamaicans. Undoubtedly this serves to establish the customary social distance, based on race, from the mainstream society. Thus, on the whole, a low entry status has traditionally been accorded to the majority of immigrants from the Caribbean. This low entry status in turn determines, in large measure, the patterns of settlement and adjustment experienced by West Indian immigrants in private and in public life. Of course, the appointment of a Lieutenant Governor, a Chancellor of a University or a Human Rights Commissioner, or the election of a couple of MPPs to Cabinet positions, all of whom are of Black or West Indian heritage, shows that the situation is by no means static. Yet, in the overall picture, it must be noted that, along with Native Canadians, Blacks and Caribbeans share the lowest levels in Canadian society. A few examples will suffice.

Caribbean youth are the victims of a streaming and tracking system in the schools which sees them disproportionately represented in terminal vocational and similar program offerings for so-called "low achievers." Several studies[31] have pointed to high expectation levels among these students followed by lower performance and achievement levels. These studies have pointed, too, to the intervening variable of an insensitive school system.

Contemporary social concern about the escalating spread and frequency of substance abuse among young people in general, and devising ways of curbing it, has resulted in disproportionate emphasis on and attention to Black, Caribbean and other visible minority groups as alleged principal perpetrators of certain types of drug related crime. The public issue concerning so-called "Black crime" has focussed attention on the question of the collection and use of crime statistics according to the ethno-cultural background of suspects.[32] Is the practice a legitimate pursuance of the duties of police officers and the police establishment? And even if it may be, have propriety and desirability considerations been carefully examined in balance with the many other issues of Black and Caribbean community/Police relations? It is at best a feeble Caribbean community response, which does not take into consideration the finding of satisfactory answers to these and many other questions.

An examination of the process of workforce adjustment of Caribbean-Canadian workers reveals that the principle of equal pay for work of equal value is being violated in both ethnic and gender terms. This inequity is a critical additional factor affecting the stability of the Caribbean family, already reeling beneath the blows of serial immigration patterns and culture shock. In demographic statistics, "dependency ratio" is the expression that means the proportion of people participating in the workforce as against those not involved in the workforce (including pre-school age and school-age children and senior citizens). For Caribbean immigrants between 1967 and 1980 this ratio rose from 0.30 to 0.80 before levelling out at 0.60 by 1987.[33] This indicates, at least theoretically, that an increasing percentage of the Caribbean community (the non-working section) has to be supported by a decreasing percentage of workers. When it is recognized that the large majority of Caribbean workers are salary and wage earners (not self-employed in construction or other business enterprises) the realization dawns that a high dependency ratio is coupled with a narrow economic base within the ethno-cultural group. This means that the effort to sustain itself as a group (for example, to provide welfare for its senior citizens and a cultural centre for the group) is fraught with difficulties. The media image of Blacks and Caribbeans is still heavily biased to sport and dance as against other creative and professional activities. A casual look at Share, a leading community weekly, would quickly confirm this.

And so, like so many other groups, the Caribbeans in Canada are faced with a powerful agenda of challenges. The reader who is struck by the colour and glamour of tourist brochures and other such literature about the Caribbean needs to think of this as well: a people's identity is a people's strength. In turn, a people's strength is measured by its collective will, which can galvanize the group to penetrate psychological as well as external barriers that limit their fullest participation in the society of their adoption. This is what self-image, self-worth and self-esteem are about. A common identity is about putting the mechanisms together to effectively serve these ends.

Sometimes I think that the poet's vision quoted at the beginning of this chapter is not very different from the "Illusions of Loveliness"[34] that Caribana features annually, or the focus of the Black media, constantly slanted towards the expressive culture needs at the expense of the instrumental power needs of the Caribbean community. For those of us who do believe that we have already lived multiculturalism, we shall have to let the inflorescence of our deeds within our own communities quicken the pace of the cross-fertilization which alone will give reality to such lofty slogans as "Unity in Diversity" or "Out of Many One People."[35] In the meantime, here are some provocative and useful questions to ponder: How is it that two societies, Canada and the Caribbean, sharing such a strong common background in history, find this background not very helpful in facilitating the process of integration, once they have come to live together as citizens of Canada? Also, is the Australian-Canadian situation, or the New Zealand-Canadian experience, or the South African-Canadian experience for that matter, similar? And then what happens when this interface of cultural collectivities happens to take place in Tobago or "The Barbados" or St. Lucia? Does race transcend culture? Under what conditions and circumstances does culture not transcend race? Answers to these questions are basic to understanding the story of the Caribbean experience in Canada.

ENDNOTES

1. This delightful poem by Allister Macmillan appears as Lesson 9 in J.O. Cutteridge's *Nelson's West Indian Readers*, Book 3, Thomas Nelson and Sons Ltd., London, 1949, p. 40.

2. *Ibid.*, p. 43.

3. For a fuller discussion of the relationship between 'mother countries' and their colonies, and the staple products which formed the economic basis of that relationship, see Eric E. Williams, *Columbus to Castro*, and George Beckford, *Persistent Poverty*.

4. In economic terms, the plantation economy was simply an overseas extension of the metropolis. See George Beckford, *op. cit.*, pp. 44-46.

5. Harold Innis, *The Fur Trade in Canada: An Introduction to Canadian Economic History*. Toronto, 1930. It is generally agreed that the pioneering work on staples theory was produced by Innis. But there have been many other contributors in the field from Canada, and other areas where the colonial experience has been shared. Relevant discussion appears in: W.I. Easterbrook and M.H. Watkins, *Approaches to Canadian Economic History*, McClelland and Stewart, 1967; Gustavus Myers, *A History of Canadian Wealth*, Lewis and Samuel, 1972; and Kari Levitt and Allister McIntyre, *Canada-West Indies Economic Relations*, 1967.

6. Erving Goffman, *Asylums*. Doubleday, New York, 1961.

7. George Beckford, *op. cit.* See also Orlando Patterson, *Sociology of Slavery*, ch. 2 and Eric Williams, *op. cit.*, chs. 9 and 10.

8. Elsa Goveia, *Slave Society in the British Leeward Islands at the end of the Eighteenth Century*, Yale University Press, 1965.

9. For further discussion see Franklin Knight, *The Caribbean*, ch. 5.

10. *Ibid.*, p. 105.

11. For accounts of slavery in Canada see: Robin Winks, *The Blacks in Canada*, Yale University Press, 1971; Vincent D'Oyley, *Black Presence in Multi-Ethnic Canada*, Ontario Institute for Studies in Education (OISE), 1976; and Daniel Hill, *The Freedom-Seekers: Blacks in Early Canada*, Book Society of Canada 1981.

12. See Easterbrook and Watkins, *op. cit.*, Part 1, p. 49ff.

13. See Robin Winks, *op. cit.* Also, Laura Foner and Eugene Genovese, *Slavery in the New World*, Prentice Hall, 1969.

14. David Lowenthal's *West Indian Societies*, O.U.P., 1972, conducts an insightful, if not always accurate, discussion of the very complex phenomena of race, colour and class in the Caribbean. A series of four volumes edited by himself and Lambros Comitas provide even more comprehensive treatment of these and allied issues over the period from emancipation into independence. All four were published in 1973 by Anchor Books under the general rubric, *West Indian Perspectives*. The specific titles are: *Slaves, Free Men and Citizens; Work and Family Life; Consequences of Class and Colour;* and *The Aftermath of Sovereignty*.

15. John Porter, *The Vertical Mosaic*, University of Toronto Press, 1965.

16. David Lowenthal, *op. cit.*, 1972.

17. These words are the last line of a poem by Edward Shirley entitled "Children of the Empire" and contained in Cutteridge's *Nelson's West Indian Readers*, Book 111, p. 200.

18. Excerpt of a classroom exchange in the author's third year course entitled "The Caribbean Experience in Multicultural Canada." February 10, 1989.

19. In the first half of the sixteenth century, Spanish conquistadors such as Hernando Cortez and Francisco Pizarro had slaughtered the Mayas and Aztecs of Mexico and the Incas of Peru in the grim process of setting up vice-royalties in the name of Spain and laying the foundations of an Iberio-Amerindian civilization. At the end of the century, Sir Walter Raleigh is making the first English contact with Trinidad and the Guianas in a vain search for Manoa, the mythical

city of gold, and its king El Dorado. The reference is to these twin circumstances which seem to symbolize and to characterize the origins of Caribbean societies. On the one hand is slaughter and domination, on the other hand, adventurism for exploitation and gain. Both images portend disaster.

20. See Edward Kamau Brathwaite, *The Development of Creole Society in Jamaica, 1770-1820*, O.U.P., London, 1971. In particular, chapter 3, 'Folk Culture of the Slaves.'

21. "Uncle Tom" is a character of self-effacing obedience referred to in generalized application to the American and West Indian slave experience. "Kunte Kinte" is a character of rigid defiance made popular in Alex Haley's *Roots*.

    Both, of course, are stereotypes which call to mind the burning debate between the Herskovitts and the Frazier schools in regard to what is myth and what is fact in the impact of slavery upon the "Negro Past."

22. Two titles by Rex Nettleford are particularly relevant to this discussion of cultural dynamics in the Caribbean. They are: *Caribbean Cultural Identity*, Institute of Jamaica, 1978, and *Mirror, Mirror: Identity, Race and Protest in Jamaica*, Collins Sangster (Jamaica) Ltd., 1972.

23. "Pitchy Patchy" was a colourful folk character in West Indian, 'Jonkonnu' masquerade bands. His costume was a multi-coloured, multi-layered outfit fashioned from strips of cloth and paper left over from the making of dresses and other costumes. He wore a hat, a tie and a mask, all in a bright array of raggy cloth and paper ends that swirled and dangled around in exaggerated exuberance as he danced. Originally, it was a way of lampooning the pomp and foppery of the slave master.

24. Frederick I. Case, *The Crisis of Identity*, Editions Naaman, 1985.

25. Gordon Lewis, *Main Currents in Caribbean Thought*, Johns Hopkins, 1983.

26. Michael G. Smith, *The Plural Society in the British West Indies*, O.U.P., 1965.

27. Leo Despres, *Cultural Pluralism and Nationalist Politics in British Guiana*, O.U.P., 1967.

28. Both Valsayn and Maraval are middle/upper class residential districts in Port-of-Spain, Trinidad.

29. A relatively recent collection of essays compiled by Simeon Chilungu and Sada Niang, entitled *African Continuities* and published by

Terebi, provides a good basis and approach towards embracing such a program of studies.

30. Freda Hawkins, *Canada and Immigration: Public Policy and Public Concern*, McGill University Press, 1972, pp. 92-93.

31. Two examples of such studies are: Agnes Calliste, "Educational and Occupational Expectations of High School Students: The Effects of Socio-Economic Background, Ethnicity and Sex." Unpublished Ph.D. Thesis, OISE, 1980, and Christopher Beserve, "Relationship Between Home Environment and Cognitive and Personality Characteristics of Working Class West Indian Pupils in Toronto." Unpublished Ph.D. Thesis, OISE, 1976.

32. The collection and use of ethno-cultural crime statistics by the police has been an issue in the public eye since the summer of 1991. It became a critical political issue in the election for mayor of the city of Toronto in November of that year.

33. This issue is given full treatment in Part 2 (ch. 5) of this monograph.

34. Frequently appearing in Caribana parades in Toronto is a float entitled "Illusions of Loveliness." It is a spectacular portrayal of brightly coloured butterflies in frolic under the golden sunshine. It was actually the winning float one year. Yet, one could hardly miss the allegorical comment on the West Indian condition.

35. These are national mottoes that appear respectively on the Canadian and Jamaican Coat-of-Arms, indicating the perceived cultural pluralism in both societies. A similar perception is somewhat more disguised in the Guyanese motto which says, "One People, One Nation, One Destiny."

CHAPTER 2

WHO ARE THE CARIBBEAN-CANADIANS?

The historical forces which informed and directed Europe's mercantilist embrace of the New World in the post-Columbus period provided a similarity of circumstances in which both Canadian and the Caribbean societies originated and emerged. From these earliest times, the frequency of communication and contact between Canada and the Caribbean has ebbed and flowed with the dictates of British colonial policies and necessities. Political and social circumstances have changed but the process has remained unbroken. The waves of post-World War II immigration from the Caribbean into Canada mark merely a new phase in the intensification of a relationship which has spanned the seventeenth, eighteenth and nineteenth centuries. In just about two generations since the start of the Domestic Scheme,[1] Caribbean peoples have come in annual waves of thousands and tens of thousands to settle in Canada.

Who are these Caribbean peoples who have been coming to reside in Canada in great numbers over the past three decades? How do their immigrant flows compare with those from other sources of Canadian migrants? What territories have they been coming from and in what numbers? What are some of the basic demographic and cultural features that characterize them? Do they constitute a coherent and distinct ethno-cultural group? And what has been the nature of their experience as they seek to integrate in their new country of adoption?

It is not the intention in this and subsequent chapters to provide full answers to all of these questions. The information that will be provided starts with a working definition of the Caribbean, briefly drawing attention to its cultural composition and complexity. This will be followed by an examination of some socio-demographic characteristics of Caribbean immigrant inflows within the context of emerging Canadian immigration policy. Further, the empirical data provided will be assessed in terms of the implications they hold for the socio-cultural adjustment of Caribbean immigrants.

From an all-inclusive perspective, however, it must be pointed out that the information that will be presented in Part 2 derives from a somewhat restricted (selected) data base. The statistical tables give information that relates to the flow situation in so far as that can be revealed by annual immigration statistics. No information is provided on natural increase through the net influence of births and deaths. Nor is there contained therein information from census sources which might have provided a fuller stock and flow picture of Caribbean-Canadians. The assumption in this strategy has been that because of the comparatively short time since the coming of these immigrants in large numbers, the socio-cultural characteristics of Caribbean-Canadians would be portrayed largely in the inflows and would not yet be significantly changed by those born in Canada. In other words, the stock is substantially, in quality if not so much so in quantity, derivative of the flow. Besides, because of shortcomings in the method of collection and presentation, data from the censuses of 1971, 1981 and 1991 are of suspect accuracy in respect to the socio-demographic features of the Caribbean community in the country. Much of this is due to complications presented by an undifferentiated use of the English mother tongue category and an unsophisticated application of the rubric "Black" to denote otherwise complicated and differentiated ethnic origins and backgrounds.

From a geographical point of view, the Caribbean proper is that archipelago of island territories stretching from Florida on the southern tip of North America to Venezuela and the Guyanas on the northern coast of South America. It includes the islands of the Greater Antilles and those of the Windward and Leeward parts of the Lesser Antilles. This chain of islands separates the Atlantic Ocean from the Caribbean Sea. Technically, the Caribbean does not include the mainland territories of Central America, but frequently Guyana on the South American mainland and Belize (formerly British Honduras) are included when reference is made to the English-speaking Caribbean.

Historically, British colonial interests determined that the area would provide a meeting ground for European, African, Asian and Amerindian civilizations. This reality has provided strong commonalities among the peoples who are today the products of that historical process. Ethno-culturally, however, there have been considerable ambiguity and confusion based on the conflicts and contradictions that flow from ascriptive and self-definitive approaches to ethnicity and identity. The differences in the ways Caribbean peoples perceive and identify themselves are as varied as the proclivity among outsiders to stereotype them is strong. The ambiguity is by no means lessened by the range of linguistic, religious, political, social and ideological forms which exist in the area. In addition to the four European-based languages— English, Spanish, French and Dutch—each of which is deemed official in its respective areas of the region, there is a rich variety of creolese and patois variants by which groups communicate in much of their daily lives. In terms of constitutional status, Caribbean territories range from independence to varying forms of 'associate statehood' with a European 'mother-country.' Political forms include one-party as well as two- and multi-party systems. Racial and ethnic diversity as well as class consciousness in these societies make for variegated patterns of cultural pluralism and a complex social structure. Ideologically, if not constitutionally, various types of capitalist democracy and socialist systems have existed, leading to what some analysts would acclaim as significant differences in life styles, world view and national and personal identities. Others would assert with equal certainty that this is a theoretical rather than a practical view. Generally, we will need to be less 'either/or' and more inclusive in our approach.

In any case, the Caribbean from which immigrants come to Canada is indeed a cultural mosaic. The ethno-cultural presence of the Caribbean in Canada provides no less a picture than a mosaic within a mosaic. This point becomes critical both for those within the Caribbean groups for whom questions of diversity and identity are persistent and obstinate, and for outsiders whose careless ascription of racial and ethnic unity often confuses the part for the whole—(Jamaica for the Caribbean) or one stereotype for complex characterizations (e.g., all Caribbean people are black).

The category "Caribbean" used by Immigration Statistics, produced by Employment, Manpower and Immigration Canada, is quite specific (and consistent after 1973). It includes the following 25 territories and 4 linguistic groupings:

English Speaking (18):

Anguilla, Antigua and Barbuda, Bahamas Islands, Barbados,

Bermuda, Cayman Islands, Dominica, Grenada, Jamaica, Montserrat, Nevis, St. Kitts, St. Lucia, St. Vincent, Trinidad and Tobago, Turks and Caicos, British Virgin Islands, American Virgin Islands

French Speaking (3):

Guadeloupe, Haiti, Martinique

Spanish Speaking (3):

Cuba, Dominican Republic, Puerto Rico

Dutch Speaking (1):

Netherland Antilles

For the purpose of this work the expression "Caribbean" includes, in addition, the four mainland territories Belize and Guyana (English speaking), French Guiana (French speaking) and Surinam (Dutch speaking). It is these 29 territories that provide the constituents of that collectivity of immigrants referred to in this work as Caribbean-Canadians.

To end this short chapter an important point needs to be underscored. It is that the expression "Black," as frequently applied to people from the Caribbean, is grossly inaccurate. Two reasons will suffice. In the first place, "Black" refers to the biological correlates of race and colour; and not all West Indians possess the same biological properties. Second, race and colour may be important, but not sufficient, factors in determining the ethnicity of a people — how they think and behave; how they view the world; how they esteem themselves. The pigmentation or colour spectrum for Caribbean-Canadians ranges from white (Europeans and Euro-Americans) through an intricate pattern of gradations and mixtures to black (from Africa and its diaspora). The colonial history which accounts for this 'rainbow' phenomenon provided as well that the path to respectability and success for the majority of these people in the Caribbean 'periphery' has been through education in the language and culture of the metropolitan societies who held them in tutelage. It is, to a large extent, this fact that explains, exogenously at any rate, Caribbean identity and personality. Fundamentally, as pointed out in Lowenthal's *West Indian Societies*, this has also meant that success has been measured "in the smaller societies by the degree of assimilation to the greater."[2] As we shall see later, one palpable contradiction of this in continuing Canadian-Caribbean relations is that the education and culture which account for the comparatively high success rate of Caribbeans in the criterion-referenced immigration entry test does not seem to hold up at the point of seeking entry into 'preferred' sectors of the workforce. Can it mean that the readiness to denote all West Indians as Blacks makes it easier to apply discrimination based on race? Succeeding chapters will cast some light on this question.

ENDNOTES

1. See footnote 2, Chapter 4.
2. See Philip Mason's Foreword in David Lowenthal's *West Indian Societies*. Oxford University Press, 1972, pp. viii-ix.

CHAPTER 3

THE SOCIO-HISTORICAL CONTEXT
OF CARIBBEAN-CANADIAN RELATIONS
AND IMMIGRATION

SOCIO-HISTORICAL CONTEXT

Professor Wilson Head, in his 1981 multicultural study entitled *Adaptation of Immigrants: Perceptions of Ethnic and Racial Discrimination*,[1] uncovered a rather interesting phenomenon: The majority of West Indian immigrants in the sample he used, when asked their reasons for immigrating, responded that it was to "seek for adventure." When compared with the other, more practical response, categories supplied by his design, such as "to seek a better economic future" or "better educational opportunities," seeking for adventure appears quite baffling—that is, until we ponder the origin and nature of Caribbean societies and the historical forces which have shaped their emergence, growth and destiny. Professor Head speculated that perhaps his question was too vague. But there might be an equally plausible thesis which suggests that the response may be quite in keeping with a characteristic or nature derived from historical circumstances. Let us look at this for a while.

In the early sixteenth century, the Christian conscience of Bishop Bartholom de las Casas,[2] protector of the Indians, was stung to sensitivity at the process of progressive genocide which European economic necessity had perpetrated on the Amerindians of the New World. So much so, indeed, that immolation and atonement for all christendom was deemed to be found in an even more brutal chapter of the *mission civilatrice*—the capture and enslavement of Blacks from Africa to work on the plantations of the Caribbean. In whatever corner of the debate one finds oneself in the Eric Williams thesis[3] which argues that slavery was the result, not of racial prejudice, but of economic necessity, the self-serving duplicity of the Catholic Church of the day in support of the las

Casas formula remains both palpable and a crime against humanity still to be redressed.

In the two centuries that led to the emancipation of the slaves in 1834, the horrors of plantation slavery, with its mono-cultural economy, its caste-like society, harsh slave laws, and near-total institutions, characterized the coming and sojourning of Africans in the Caribbean. At all times and in all ways they were slaves, not masters, of the land to which they were brought. It was a classic interplay and struggle between economic and political forces; mercantile, industrial and landed interests; and upper, middle and working classes which brought about the emancipation of slaves in 1834. Humanitarianism had little to do with it.[4] But the slaves themselves, by revolts and a growing awareness and restiveness, helped to promote the condition in which the passing of the Act became inevitable.

But emancipation did not quell the insatiable hunger of the plantation system for cheap labour. In fact, it may well have increased it. Thus, the ensuing years of indentureship were to see other groups of immigrant servants pressed into service under the Caribbean sun. These people, in the chronological order in which they came, comprised Portuguese from Madeira, Chinese from mainland China and Hong Kong, and East Indians from southern and eastern India.[5] In addition, a pattern of internal migration developed as ex-slaves from over-worked and debt burdened plantations, in islands such as Barbados, St. Kitts and Antigua were induced to move south and east to Guyana and Trinidad where fresher soils and more modern technology promised greater profitability from sugar for the planter class. These, then, were the newcomers, the wage labourers, to take the place of the former African and Creole slaves[6] who now, with their new status as free men, could choose, and in many cases did choose, to move completely away from the plantation, or to give their labour there only when they so desired. The Portuguese and the Chinese did not labour long on the sugar plantations. They soon found their way into small shopkeeping businesses. East Indian indentured labourers immigrated into the Caribbean well into the second decade of the twentieth century. The terms of their indentureship reserved them to harsh plantation labour. They too were made to sing "the Lord's song in a strange land."[7]

These, then, were the immigrant peoples who, together with some later arrivals from the Middle East, in the twentieth century were to provide the demographic base of the English-speaking Caribbean in particular. It needs to be further emphasized, however, that over both the pre- and post-emancipation periods, as Caribbean society emerged, characteristic elements of the process were duress and reluctance. The Africans were forcibly wrested from their tribes, their culture, their kinship patterns and their families. The indentured Asians, both east and south, shared a process of physical and cultural uprooting that was, at best, a trifle better than the slavery it replaced. It is hardly to be expected, then, that such an historical experience would breed any deep sense of psycho-social belonging within and among Caribbean people. On the contrary, it would be understandable for a people to be pre-disposed to flee the locus of their oppression and torture. And when there is no 'homeland,' no 'bantustand' to which they may readily return, wanderlust may well ensue and migratory tendencies become characteristic.

It is in this context that Wilson Head's "seeking for adventure" comes into the picture in a subliminally expressive sense—particular to an indigenously displaced people. When the definitive program of research and analysis has come to be done, the Caribbean may not, in the perception of many domiciled there, be 'home.' It may, instead, be merely the latest stop in the epic journey of an uprooted and unsettled people. This assertion is not lightly made. The author is perfectly aware that this picture, this perspective of the West Indian as an unsettled, homeless migrant, stricken with wanderlust over the centuries, is hardly likely, at first blush, to do much more than shock the reader and offend the sensitivities and pride of fellow West Indians. Let it be readily acknowledged. The studies of identity, self-awareness and self-esteem of West Indians, both as a nation and at the personal level, have not yet been done to lend authentication to this thesis or, for that matter, to dismiss it. But the very process of conjecture and self-analysis from which a valid grasp of who or what is the West Indian personality may come, stands impoverished if the posing and investigation of such theories is squelched on the altar of so-called Caribbean good name and respectability.

Yet, it is not as though we were in a situation of no information at all. To begin, there is a pretty strong body of evidence to support the claim of a migratory tendency among West Indian men in particular—at least since the early twentieth century. Included on a list of such evidence would be the post-1917 back to India movement as the indentureship process came to an end. A similar back to Africa sentiment and supportive action has pervaded Afro-Caribbean history: the Maroons (to Nova Scotia then to Sierra Leone), teachers to South Africa, the Marcus Garvey movement, the Pan-African movement and more recent Rastafarian sequels. Among Sino-Caribbeans, the back to

China/Hong Kong movement has not been well known; but the small trickle of persons immigrating to Canada from Hong Kong[8] who give as their place of birth some territory in the Caribbean—usually Jamaica, Surinam or Guyana—provide evidence of some migratory trend among Chinese-Caribbeans as well.

At the turn of the twentieth century, during the Panama Canal period and after, the migratory trend intensified. The chronicle of movement of Caribbean male workers included a range of skills to be used in the Canal zone and the sugar and banana plantations of Panama, Costa Rica, Cuba and the U.S.[9] In fact, these men were to become the precursors of much larger and more regular waves of human resources to leave the Caribbean in search of economic betterment in the U.S., the U.K. and Canada in the post-World War II years. The magnitude of Caribbean migration to these territories and elsewhere in modern times marks merely a crescendo in a movement that is the characteristic by-product of the process and experience of colonial exploitation. But we cannot now follow this line of thought much further.

We have prepared the way for a brief and focussed look at the question of 'push-pull' factors in the immigration process, and it is to this issue that we must now turn.

'Push-pull' factors in immigration include the many conditions and circumstances which motivate people to leave one country for life in another. These conditions are political, economic and social in nature, each aspect presenting a constellation of features and circumstances often inter-related and complex, but applicable in some cases while not in others. The convention refugee, for example, who fears for his safety in, or safe return to, his country of birth (or of last permanent residence) because of actions or threats from a political party or administration in power, experiences a push factor away from that country. As another example, the quest for improved working and living opportunities, for whatever reason impossible in a home country, can constitute a set of economic and psychological push factors that stimulates the potential emigrant to search for a better future abroad. Absence of access to educational and medical opportunities can also present the motivating factors for seeking a better life outside one's country of birth or last permanent residence. Complementary with each of these categories of push factors there stands a set of pull factors which will help determine the country to which the emigrant presents himself/herself for betterment. Pull factors, then, are the conditions and circumstances which the host or receiving society knowingly or inadvertently extends to the potential newcomer. Immigration laws and regulations which indicate attractive entry conditions and hold promise of the assurance of the candidate's status after entry are good examples of effective pull factors. In turn, these factors may have a lot to do with economic, labour market, moral and ethical considerations at the core of the philosophic outlook of the country. Another powerful pull factor is often provided by the presence in the host society of large numbers of relatives and friends of potential emigrants from the presenting society.

Let us understand that none of these generalizations speaks adequately to any one situation, least of all, perhaps, to the Caribbean-Canadian case. In reference specifically to the Caribbean and Canada, a number of colonial and neo-colonial factors have controlled the overall context of relationships that they have shared and from which migratory, push-pull factors have derived. Over the centuries since the post-Columbian, European embrace of the New World, Canada and the Caribbean have both filled roles as the 'periphery' in relation to European metropolitan 'centres.' And, to a much lesser extent, the Caribbean area has served as Canada's hinterland. The mercantilist logic of economic nationalism dictated that the staple products—sugar, fish, fur and timber—provide the structural design for the architecture of those societies and the nature and quality of the relationship between them. Inevitably, then, in order to understand push-pull factors between them, in the sense of contemporary migration patterns, a Weberian type of historical approach, in which understanding is the painstaking result of empathy, needs to be applied. If, in the colonial period, the relationship between Britain and her colonies was basically exploitative, Canadian Confederation after 1867 merely lessened the degree of that exploitation. Political independence, when it finally came to the Caribbean in the 1960s, proved incapable of eradicating an economic and cultural dependency that had been deftly orchestrated from abroad, and that had become endemic and deep-seated at home. Consequently, the determining force behind push-pull factors in Caribbean-Canadian immigration relations, though deep and strong in history, was indirect and halting precisely because of that history. Really, the determining force behind these push-pull factors was a policy of economic nationalism in which each colony shared direct trade relations with the mother country, while inter-relations among colonies happened indirectly, through mediation of the mother country. Robin Winks' *Forty Year Minuet*[10] and Robert Chodos' *Caribbean Connections*[11] are two of the many sources that provide ample details of the twentieth century picture of Caribbean-Canadian inter-relationships. The former emphasized the commercial basis of these relationships while the latter presents a more broad-based account reflecting the perspectives of a number of disciplines.

To go a little beyond these efforts is to point out that while the focus in the Caribbean-Canadian relationship up to World War II was on the exploitation of physical resources, in the decades since the 1960s human resources have become the focal point of this relationship.[12] It would not be an overstatement to say that 'King Sugar' has lost considerable ground to the new imperative of the human capital concept—the investment potential of the skills embodied in human resources.

The triangular trade relations which existed among Europe, Africa and the Caribbean over the mercantilist centuries enabled the commodity sugar to become king, and established a climate of international relations in which a particular push-pull dynamic determined the basis of commodity and resource movement. Before the emancipation of the slaves, the third leg of the triangle started in the Caribbean and ended in the ports of Bristol and Liverpool in England, with the principal commodity being sugar and its by-products, rum and molasses.[13] In the post-emancipation years, however, and particularly after the free trade movement in the second half of the nineteenth century, America and Canada became significant terminal points of commodity movement from the Caribbean. Then, in the post-World War II period, resource movement from the Caribbean to Britain, the U.S. and Canada came increasingly to include a component of human resources. Sugar was still important, but it was no longer 'king.' Categories of trained and experienced manpower embodying a range of technical and other skills and expertise had become the prime commodity which traditionally imperialist, exploitative Atlantic-Caribbean relations now required.

World War II had taken the customary toll war takes on human lives. The toll on the lives of young males in particular, was heavy. Thus, post-war national redevelopment policies began to emphasize, in Canada as they did in the U.S. and other developed societies, manpower and human resource requirements. Assessment of human resource stock and flow began to disclose an increasing level of importance of middle- and upper-level skill needs as well as projected ranges of secondary, post-secondary and on-the-job training measures to meet these needs. Among other strategies for filling the perceived manpower requirements if economic growth were to be stimulated and sustained was immigration. And this became even more imperative after the late 1950s. The challenge to Western societies posed by the successful launching of Sputnik by Russia in 1957 served to intensify the emphasis, in these nations, on the provision and acquisition of technical and technological skills. Institutional training for the provision of these skills was deemed a necessary long-run, but not a sufficient short-run, approach to solving the problem.[14] Therefore, appropriately trained and experienced human resources had to be obtained from abroad.

In the case of Canada, the geographical areas from which such human resources were to come included, by the late 1960s, the Caribbean. It was within this context and from this background that the demand and supply of skilled manpower became a powerful factor in the push-pull relationship between Canada and the Caribbean. The Canadian labour force needed the skills. This was the pull factor. The Caribbean was over-supplied with skilled workers who, because of the under-developed state of their own economies, were forced to leave their homelands. This was the push factor. As we shall see later, the changes in Canadian immigration policy in 1962 and 1967 provided the political linkage for push-pull factors to emerge into larger waves of Caribbean immigration into Canada. But this is to move ahead somewhat too quickly.

In so far as the potential Caribbean emigrant is concerned, the push factor that impels him/her to emigrate to Canada is the opportunity to improve conditions, economic and otherwise, for his/her family. But from our overall analytical point of view, this so-called economic opportunity is a complex factor. It consists of political, social and psychological ramifications, all emanating from deep-rooted historical circumstances indelibly etched in the psyche of the 'indigenous migrant' discussed in reference to Wilson Head's "seeker of adventure."

The economic determinism of the plantation system not only enriched Europe and North America at the expense of the Caribbean, but it also inflicted deep psychological wounds on both colonizer and colonized. And, according to Fanon,[15] the post-colonial national bourgeoisie in these territories became merely the compradors and handmaidens of continued colonial exploitation. Thus, the extent and degree of "immiseration" experienced in the post-World War II plantation Caribbean provided ample leaven for escalating emigration from them. Because of the dependency links that developed between colonized and colonizer, it is not strange that places like Britain and Canada became popular with would-be Caribbean emigrants. For similar reasons, it is not difficult to understand how human resources have come to surpass sugar as the principal export commodity from the sunny Caribbean islands "smiling still in tempest and in calm."[16]

Until 1962, Britain and the U.S. were the principal emigrant destinations for the Caribbean. But in that year a number of events and circumstances in all three areas coincided to make Canada, thereafter, the principal country of choice for Caribbean emigrants. In Britain, it was the ending of the 'open-door' immigration policy that had traditionally existed between the 'mother country' and her 'commonwealth dependencies.' As colonial subjects of the British Empire, Caribbean citizens were British subjects who enjoyed the right to carry a British passport and to enter, work in and settle in Britain with ease. But this status did not confer the same freedom of entry into the Dominions such as Canada, Australia or New Zealand. In the post-war 1950s this right was more frequently exercised. The influx of West Indians into Britain grew rapidly, and, as was demonstrated by the Notting Hill Riots of 1956,[17] race relations tensions began to surface in urban and industrial areas where settlement of West Indian and other visible minority newcomers was most dense. In the face of these domestic British circumstances and the continuing political winds of change that blustered over the British Commonwealth and Empire, the Commonwealth Immigrants Act was passed in 1962.[18] The effect of this Act was to remove from West Indians the "right" to enter, work in and settle in Britain and to replace it with a "privilege" underwritten by a Ministry of Labour employment voucher. The fact that this new situation did not apply to West Indians alone, but to other members of the Commonwealth and Empire as well, did not lessen the degree of hardship posed for expectant Caribbean emigrants.

The second set of events to happen in 1962 that was to have significant influence on the patterns of relationship and immigration between Canada and the Caribbean revolved around the granting of political independence, first to Jamaica on August 6, and then to Trinidad and Tobago on August 31. The changed status of these two territories was naturally accompanied by a number of political and diplomatic ramifications. For example, both these new countries could now confer the status of citizenship on their nationals, issue their own passports and establish diplomatic relations with Canada, including the negotiating of mutually agreed immigration approaches. It should be noted, as well, that while the conferring of Caribbean nationhood through the act of political independence may have brought great pride to some elements of the multi-racial, multi-ethnic populace in these societies, it could not and did not guarantee the instant transformation of economic and socio-cultural circumstances which would have curbed the growing tendency towards emigration. Indeed, for some, independence might well have provided the impetus to move out.

The third factor which made 1962 the critical year in the development of the pattern of immigration relations between the Caribbean and Canada was the passing, in February, of the 1962 Regulations of the Canadian Immigration Act. More will be said about these Regulations shortly. But it is important to remark on two of their significant features at this point. The main intentions of these Regulations were two: first, to remove racial discrimination as a major feature of Canada's immigration policy—at least in any explicit sense; and, second, to explicitly establish skill as the main criterion in the selection of unsponsored immigrants. The first of these features acted in favour of the West Indies in two ways. Not only did it remove overt forms of selection discrimination, it also included the English-speaking Caribbean among those countries privileged to exercise the sponsorship provision from among a wider range of 'close' relatives. The skill emphasis, in its turn, presented a welcome beacon to the many graduates and others whose level of demoralization grew each day with the under-utilization of their skills and whose appetite for work and study abroad, as for any other consumer commodity, revealed a remarkable preference for that which was foreign.[19]

Thus, as the immigration door to Britain appeared to swing close, in 1962, the one to Canada appeared to swing open. The coming of political independence to Caribbean territories in that same year did not bring with it the instant life improvements promised and expected. And the 'indigenous itinerant' turned to Canada, unwittingly replacing primary products with human resources as the principal exports of a tragic dependency syndrome.

IMPACT OF CARIBBEAN IMMIGRATION POLICY ON VOLUME AND PATTERN OF CARIBBEAN IMMIGRANT INFLOWS

Caribbean immigration into Canada since World War II fits conveniently into two periods: pre-1967 and post-1967.

For both periods it is not merely the economic, political and social push factors from the Caribbean which account for the volume and pattern of immigration flows from that area. As we have seen in the previous section, these are important in themselves. But now we must turn to examine more closely the pull effect created by the somewhat dramatic emergence of Canada's immigration policy. It is this pull effect which provides the major determinant of how many Caribbean immigrants were admitted into Canada and the demographic features which characterize the inflows.

For the first analytical period ending in 1967, three signposts in the emergence of Canadian immigration policy may be isolated.[20] They are the Mackenzie King Statement of 1947 and its culmination in the Immigration Act of 1952; the 1962 Amendment to the Immigration Act which initiated a universalist policy; and the White Paper and Immigration Regulations of 1966/67 which systematized that universalist policy. For the second analytical period, from 1967 to the present, the important signposts are provided by the Green Paper discussions that engaged the nation between 1973 and 1975, and their culmination in the streamlining of immigration policy embodied in the 1978 Act. A brief sketch of what these signposts reveal as to the evolution and nature of national immigration policy and its consequent effect on immigration from the Caribbean is essential at this point.

In summary fashion we will attempt to establish that it was the progressive removal of the systematic forms of discrimination in policy, coupled with the creation of universalist criteria for immigrant selection—within the context of the absorptive capacity and priority labour force needs of Canada's economy— that immigration from the Caribbean was able to demonstrate its competitive edge and to grow rapidly. Now we must give a more detailed examination to this statement.

May 1, 1947, is an important date in the commencement of this examination. It was on that date that the Prime Minister, Mackenzie King, adumbrated his government's policy in respect to immigration. He explained that there were two central pillars of that policy. First, immigration was to be encouraged based on the absorptive capacity of Canada's economy. Second, there was to be the removal (at least in its overt forms) of "objectionable discrimination"[21] in that policy. As a result of these considerations and their embodiment in the Immigration Act of 1952, it became possible for Canada to enter into that kind of agreement with Caribbean territories out of which annual quotas of domestic workers provided the first systematic flow of immigrants after 1955.

The second signpost of development in Canadian immigration policy came with the amendment of the Immigration Act in 1962. With the amendment, emphasis on "preferred nationalities" was reduced while that on the perceived economic and occupational needs of Canada was increased. Policy moved significantly away from overt discrimination towards universal applicability of the same admission criteria, namely, "education, training, skills or other special qualifications."[22] As a result, for the first time, Caribbean citizens were able to enter Canada as unsponsored or independent immigrants.

The third development in the evolution of Canadian immigration policy which facilitated Caribbean immigration is identifiable in the White Paper Recommendations of 1966 and the 1967 Regulations which followed from them. The White Paper had paid much attention to the moral issues such as family unification and the giving of assistance to refugees and the less privileged. Its more important emphasis, however, was on the interconnection between immigration and manpower policy and, as a concomitant of that, the need to bring a total end to racial discrimination in Canadian immigration policy. In order to accomplish this, a universalist selection criterion known as the "points system" was designed and recommended. Based on these recommendations, the 1967 Regulations set in place the following provisions:

> First, discrimination on the basis of race was explicitly eliminated from official immigration policy.
>
> Second, three categories of immigrant were specified: unsponsored, or independent, nominated relatives and sponsored dependents. In order to rationalize immigrant selection through these three categories, a 9-factor system was devised against which candidates would qualify. These factors took account of both the short-term and long-term needs of the Canadian economy. There was a built-in "points system" designed to be flexibly applied so as to hold in balance these short-term and long-term needs.[23]
>
> Third, prospective immigrants were now allowed to apply for landed status under any of the three categories whilst on visit to Canada.

Fourth, an Immigration Appeal Board was created
to deal with difficulties that arose in the
administration of these regulations. It was to be
impartial and non-political.[24]

Cumulatively, these provisions had the effect of opening the doors to immigrants from the Caribbean to an unprecedented extent; and the years that followed indicate this both in terms of numbers and pattern of arrival. The trickle of immigrants, principally in lowly sectors of the workforce up to 1967, were to become, as we shall see after that year, a strong and steady flow of well-educated and highly skilled manpower in response to specified Canadian development and labour force requirements.

In 1967, the immigrant selection criteria had ostensibly been designed to remove the racist stigma associated with the doctrine of "most-preferred country status" from Canadian immigration policy and practice.[25] And this has turned out to have a profound and lasting effect on the racial, linguistic, religious and ethno-cultural mix of Canada's population. The Official Languages Act of 1969 as well as the Multicultural Statement of 1971 were events that presaged forthcoming changes in the nature of Canadian society and the pattern of immigration which continuously thereafter would transfuse its life-blood.

But, in the period since the establishment of the 1967 points system, the underlying principles of Canadian immigration policy have remained substantially the same. These principles are three: satisfying Canadian labour force requirements, having regard to the absorptive capacity thereof; concern for family unification—the landed immigrant and the close members of his/her family; and a compassionate and humanitarian concern for the displaced peoples of the world—the refugee situation. Based on these three principles, immigration policy has generally recognized a tripartite classification of immigrants over the years—the family class, the convention refugee class and the independent class. And it is around these 'classes' that the emergence of policy has moved. Moreover, and this must be carefully noted, it is within the dynamics of the changes in these areas that Caribbean migration to Canada in the decades of the 1970s and 1980s and continuinginto the 1990s can best be examined and understood.

A number of signposts of these changes can be identified, and the rest of this chapter will proceed from a discussion of these signposts and their socio-economic and political contexts. The first post-1967 situation emerged in 1973 and became known as the "Adjustment of Status Program." The 1967 Immigration Regulations had made it possible for visitors to Canada to apply for landed immigrant status whilst in Canada. By 1973, some 17,000 of such visitors were waiting for a hearing before the Immigration Appeal Board, which was the body set up by the aforesaid regulations to deal with the situation. The backlogt became so heavy that the Minister was forced to submit a Bill in the House of Commons. In it he argued that:

> The right to apply in Canada for immigrant status was a noble experiment that proved unworkable and has to be laid to rest, but I think decency demands that it be done fairly.[26]

As a result, for 60 days during the months of August and September that status adjustment, or amnesty, or "Project 97" exercise was conducted. This swelled the landed immigrant total for that year by 39,000. In Chapter 4, it will be seen that both in terms of absolute numbers and percentage of total Canadian immigration for that year, the Caribbean experienced one of its years of highest contribution.

A second signpost in the development of Canadian immigration policy that was to have a significant effect on the Caribbean inflow happened over the years 1974-1978. First some unfavourable economic and demographic developments occurred. The world-wide oil crisis of 1973 saw the price of oil in Canada escalate four-fold, which led to a serious slowdown of the economy. Coupled with that was a progressive birth rate decline in the 1960s which was beginning to slow the growth of the working-age population.[27] All of this in turn led to a reconsideration of the immigration question, the kind of review that sought to "create a new long-term basis for Canada's immigration and population policy."[28] To facilitate this nationwide process, a series of four discussion documents known collectively as the Green Paper was prepared by the Department of Manpower and Immigration and circulated. The four volumes were:

1. Immigration Policy Perspectives
2. The Immigration Program
3. Immigration and Population Statistics
4. Three Years in Canada: A Longitudinal Survey

Essentially, the intent of these documents was to have the public "ponder the future of Canada's population—its size, rate of growth, distribution and composition—and to review the principles that should govern the admission and integration of immigrants from abroad."[29] But the process failed to gain the full support of the media, who, for the most part, seemed less interested in informing and educating the public than in indulging its partisanship and prejudices. Many public sessions became heated and disrupted as sentiments became biased against the thought of an 'expansionist' immigration program. And the saddest part of it all was its eruption into a shameful pogrom of 'Paki-bashing' which characterized inter-group relations across the nation.[30]

The anticipated legislation was tabled in 1976 and proclaimed in 1978. It provided for a revised points system that gave less emphasis to the applicant's educational attainment and more to his/her occupational experience. Also, the legislation formally specified the three classes of immigrants already recognized in practice—the family class, independents and refugees. But then it sought to alter the proportion among the three: away from the family class and towards independents and refugees.

Predictably, the impact on the volume of migrants coming from the Caribbean was striking. From an average figure of 25,000 over the years 1973-1975, there was a drop to a 15,000 average between 1976 and 1978 and a further drop to about 9,000 for the years 1979 and 1980—the lowest point in the first 15 years of the series since 1966.[31] Traditionally, the family class has been the major category into which Caribbean immigrants have been placed. But over the years since 1967, a precise definition of "relatives eligible under the family class"[32] has proved elusive, causing difficulties for applicants and selection agents alike. Variously, the literature would refer to "sponsored relatives," "nominated relatives" and "assisted relatives" with equal confusion for the sponsored as well as the sponsor; and providing, at best, a lucrative new field for a new branch of entrepreneurs to become established as immigration consultants. According to the Regulations of 1978, close family members were not to be assessed under the points system. All they needed was to be of good health and character and to have the sponsoring relatives agree to guarantee them lodging and care over the first 10 years after their arrival. This kind of confusion stemming from conflicting advice between selection officers overseas (particularly the "good intentions" of visa officers in the Caribbean) and the administrative bureaucracy in Canada was one difficulty. Another was the long delays that ensued in the processing of applicants' files. Together they led to a questioning of the efficiency of the system. It was just a matter of time before further changes would be instituted.

And, sure enough, yet another movement in an evolving immigration policy was initiated in 1985. It was not a surprise either that, again, it seemed to be occasioned by a perceived correlation with Canada's economic fortunes. By 1984, Canada seemed to be recovering from the oil crises of the 1970s, but since the Act of 1978 total immigration levels had been declining. Coinciding with that was a noticeable and unsettling drop in the country's birth rate. The Minister of Employment and Immigration, in his 1985 Report to Parliament, stressed the need for an assessment of the linkage between the rate of immigration and the future size, natural rate of growth and composition of the population. This was followed by an even more specific report from the Standing Committee on Labour, Employment and Immigration of the House of Commons, recommending that:

> every effort should be made, beginning today, and continuing for at least 30 years, to consider using immigration policy to smooth out the current age imbalance in the Canadian population.[33]

Together these two reports underlined the prevailing perception that immigration should not only be tied to Canada's specific labour force needs in terms of occupational skills, but should also compensate for the fluctuations in domestic fertility rates of some 20 years earlier.[34]

In 1986 there was a change to the Regulations of 1978 in the application of the points system. The maximum number of points obtainable remained 100, but more emphasis was now to be placed on training and employment-related factors. For example, experience, practical training and education accounted for about half of the possible points assessment.[35] This revised selection criteria applied only to independents and assisted relatives.

The impact of this development on immigration levels was instant. Planning levels were raised, met, and in some cases exceeded.[36] Of greater significance, however, was the source from which the preponderance of the new immigrants were coming. They were, and have since been, coming from areas in the world where population growth and fertility rates are among the highest—for example, South and East Asia and the Caribbean.[37] In July 1988, in response to another report by the House of Commons Standing Committee on Labour, Employment and Immigration, the family definition was extended to include all never-married children and their own never-married children. This led to an unusual growth in family class immigration, and for the Caribbean, whose largest proportion of immigrants usually falls into that class, this meant a further boost in numbers. Yet, because of the overall increase in total Canadian immigration, coming largely from the heavily populated areas of Asia and the Far East, the Caribbean contribution, though growing in absolute numbers, has fallen off significantly in terms of percentage.[38]

THE REFUGEE QUESTION

An equally important aspect of Canadian immigration policy to develop over the years since World War II has been associated with the refugee question and the influence of international migration on that question. From the time of the establishment of the office of the United Nations High Commissioner for Refugees in 1950, which defined a convention refugee, to the 1967 Protocol which amended that definition, and over the years to the present, Canada has held a high profile in seeking strategies of determination of the problem at the international level as well as policy initiatives to deal with it at home. The rubric defines a convention refugee as a person who, "owing to well-founded fear of being persecuted for reasons of race, religion, nationality, membership of a particular social group or political opinion, is outside the country of his nationality and is unable, or owing to such fear, is unwilling to avail himself of the protection of that country; or who, not having a nationality and being outside the country of his former habitual residence, is unable or, owing to such fear, is unwilling to return to it." And it is quite plausible that inherent in the problem is the complication of the definition itself.

The Inter-governmental Committee for European Migration (ICEM) founded in 1951 had Canada as one of its 16 founding members. But by 1962 Canada had withdrawn from active membership. It is useful to note that ICEM was a Euro-focussed body dealing predominantly with the interests of Europeans who sought to migrate to Latin America. As such, it did little to foster interest in refugees from other parts of the world who wanted to come to Canada. By 1970, however, the knocking on Canada's own doors had become very strident and much more attention became drawn to the new claimants for refuge and asylum. They included 'strangers' from East Europe, East and North Africa, the Middle East, South Asia, the Far East, and Latin

America. But even into the 1980s refugees from the Caribbean were an inconspicuous few.

The refugee question as it relates to the Caribbean-Canadian experience became really important around 1983. The 1976 Immigration Act had set up an inland refugee determination system for the processing of claims submitted by applicants after their arrival in Canada. It was expected that that would increase the number of refugee claimants, and it did. But, regrettably, the administrative system was never equal to the task and the backlog grew worse. The phenomenon of "illegal immigrants," that is, those who came as visitors and over-stayed, or decided to remain illegally 'under-ground,' did not help matters either. Many of these were to swell the ranks of those applying as refugees from within Canada. Immigration-commissioned studies established that on a national scale the most frequent offenders as "illegal migrants" were Jamaicans, Americans, Indians, Guyanese and Portuguese in that order, and that, in Toronto, those most frequently caught and deported were from the Caribbean—Jamaica, Trinidad and Guyana in particular.[39]

The Canadian response to this situation included the imposition of a visa requirement for visitors to Canada from the most infamous illegal migrant sources. And, of course, Jamaica, Guyana and Trinidad and Tobago were among them. These visa requirements included stricter supervision at the point of entry, more precise specification of period of stay and more careful monitoring of the departure of visitors. Then, in 1986, the government undertook an Administrative Review to deal with backlogged refugee claims. It granted status to 20,300 persons who qualified as convention refugees, or who were able to demonstrate their ability to establish successfully in Canada, or who had close family members here, or who were in situations similar to refugees.[40]

It was feared, and it came to pass, that the Administrative Review would merely trigger the arrival of new refugee claimants. By 1988, there were 85,000 claimants waiting for their cases to be heard, and it is likely that visitors who were not genuine refugees may have applied for refugee status knowing full well that that would allow them to "remain in Canada as long as five years until their cases were resolved."[41]

In January 1989, a new system of refugee determination vested in an Immigration and Refugee Board was set up to help clear the backlog of refugee claims and to answer directly to Parliament. By 1992, the refugee backlog was still both unmanageable in numbers and escalating in cost. The Caribbean, particularly now Trinidad and Guyana, where race relations continue to deteriorate, have become major exponents of the game of refugee politics and have done so with considerable success. All in all, refugeeism has not, in the past, been an important factor in Caribbean migratory pattern to Canada. But, as the Canadian policy evolves, this too is changing. The refugee status determination process is still complicated and complex, if for no other reason than Canadian constitutional law and jurisprudence—the Charter of Rights and Freedoms and the tradition of court decisions supposedly allow each claimant the rights of due process and a decent living while waiting for determination. Caribbean migrants, in their turn, are sufficiently entrepreneurial not to miss an opportunity to maximize their benefits.[42]

CONCLUSION

Canadian immigration policy in the second half of the twentieth century has been a complex evolutionary process, and Caribbean migration to Canada since 1967 has moved largely in step with that process. In summarizing and commenting on the changes in Canadian policy, three important points need to be emphasized. One is the relationship that has existed between Canada's economic and demographic circumstances on the one hand, and the process of immigration on the other. A large section of public opinion has usually behaved as if the conventional wisdom is that poor economic circumstances should trigger the dampening of immigration. An examination of Canada's approach has rather revealed the opposite. It has presented empirical evidence that immigration could provide a good catalyst for stimulating economic turnarounds. The second point is that the attempts at balancing issues of economic necessity with matters of compassionate and humanitarian concerns must often preclude the formulation of policies that are too rigid. Also, the policies chosen must have the benefit of sound management and administrative systems to implement, monitor, evaluate and correct them. Third, it would seem time to realize and to act positively on the realization that immigration planning should address the need for settlement and integration services that would provide for smooth adjustment of immigrants into their adopted country and communities.

As of 1991, a five-year immigration plan (1991-1995) has been put into operation, and it is to be hoped that the overall similarity that this plan seems to bear to the three principles stated above is not merely a token of good intentions. Some twenty years ago, policy seemed to be steering in a similar direction. The first report of the longitudinal survey on the economic and

48

social adaptation of immigrants, entitled "Three Years in Canada,"[43] had indicated that, to a large extent, immigrants were able to realize the occupational intentions they held prior to arrival in Canada.[44] However, one-fifth of the immigrant sample thought that their overall social situation had deterioratedfrom what it had been in their country of origin. Further, it was found that this negative assessment was most frequent among those who were unemployed or not working in their chosen professions.[45] This provides some straight evidence of an unfortunate gap between policy and practice. Since then, some attention has been paid to improving matters in this regard. But it would be difficult to say with any degree of accuracy in what way attempts at change have been effective.[46] What can be asserted with greater certainty is that co-ordinated planning and management of immigration is still vital for Canada, and that a smooth integration into economy and society for the newcomer is the real test, the cutting edge, of the system.

The current five-year immigration plan provides for:

> a moderate increase in immigration while maintaining a reasonable balance among the family, refugee and independent categories. Immigration will rise from 200,000 in 1990 to 220,000 in 1991 and to 250,000 in 1992 where it will be stabilized for the rest of the planning periods.[47]

It is proposed that government's commitment to family reunification will remain central to the program and family-related regulations will be modified to reflect genuine dependency relationships among core family members, for example, parents, spouses, fiancé(es), grandparents and dependent children. Canada's international commitments concerning refugees will be maintained. These commitments will extend to government-assisted refugees and members of designated classes selected abroad, privately sponsored refugees, those landed in Canada after January 1989. And, resolutely, strategies to deal with them more effectively will be sought. Relative to the others, the overall proportion of skilled workers, independents and assisted relatives will be increased towards the end of the plan period in accordance with national and provincial priority skill needs.

Further, the plan proposes an annual program review by way of improving the general management of the immigration process, and to identify specific areas of focus in the succeeding five-year forward plan. In addition, a federal integration strategy is proposed which will provide, through partnerships at the federal, provincial, municipal and private corporation levels, a network of co-ordinated services to facilitate the integration of newcomers into their new communities.[48]

The ultimate question for our discussion at this point is how would all this affect future immigrant inflows from the Caribbean. Taken in the context of past interaction, the short answer must be that there will be a dramatic effect, and that that effect is likely to be towards a decline in both the absolute numbers and proportions of these numbers in relation to the total Canadian inflow. There is already evidence of this. The 1991 statistics from Immigration Canada record that of a national total of 230,781 immigrants (based on Country of Last Permanent Residence) only 16,156, or a mere 7 percent, were from the Caribbean. It would seem that for the remaining years of the current plan period it would be difficult for the Caribbean to hold, let alone improve on, its percentage of the national inflow. As pointed out earlier, the priority sources from which Canadian immigrants are currently coming include Asia and the Far East. Both labour force necessities and fertility rate factors have determined this. And the Caribbean is hardly likely, in the foreseeable future, to become one of the world's more serious refugee sources.

Thus, even though the Caribbean may continue for some time to show small increases in absolute numbers, the probability is very slight indeed that there could be a recurrence of the double-digit percentages it contributed for some years in the 1970s and 1980s. But there is a positive side to this. While Caribbean immigration numbers are low, we should take the opportunity to focus our attention on the effective integration of more of the Caribbeans who are already here and to prepare additional supportive structures for those who are yet to come. For the leaders of the ethno-cultural community, perhaps this is the time to begin to mobilize for massive responses to the challenges of integration and settlement with and/or without the assistance of government and other private agencies. The group must define the task as one that starts with the emergence of critical consciousness and then proceeds along such lines as those sketched out in Appendix 3.

ENDNOTES

1. Wilson Head, *Adaptation of Immigrants: Perceptions of Ethnic and Racial Discrimination*. York University, 1981, pp. 91ff.

2. For a brief account of the role of Bishop Bartholom de las Casas among the Indians, see Eric Williams, *From Columbus to Castro: The History of the Caribbean 1492 to 1969*. Andre Deutsch, 1970, pp. 34-37, 43-45.

3. Eric Williams in his *Capitalism and Slavery* enunciates this thesis, which has been very closely debated by scholars of West Indian history. See chapter 1 of the present volume. See also Max Ifill, *The African Diaspora*. Economic and Business Research, Port-of-Spain, Trinidad, pp. 11-20.

4. Eric Williams, *op. cit.* See, in particular, his chapter entitled "The Saints and Slavery."

5. See Keith O. Laurence, *Immigration into the West Indies in the 19th Century*. Caribbean United Press, Barbados, 1971.

6. Orlando Patterson's *The Sociology of Slavery* provides one of the best-known sources for understanding the creolization process that ensues.

7. Biblical reference to the Jewish story of captivity.

8. Evidence of this is reported in Canadian Immigration Statistics. In Table 14, which crosses Country of Last Permanent Residence with Country of Birth, evidence of this appears for the years 1979, 1980, 1981, 1982 and 1983. This evidence does not appear in subsequent years.

9. For a full discussion of the destinations, volume and chronology of these immigrant waves see R. Greenwood and S. Hamber, *Emancipation to Emigration*. Macmillan Caribbean, 1990.

10. Robin Winks, *Canadian-West Indian Union: A Forty-Year Minuet*. Commonwealth Papers #11, University of London, Athlone Press, 1968.

11. Robert Chodos, *The Caribbean Connection*. James Lorimer and Co., Toronto, 1977.

12. The socio-demographic discussion in Part 11 will illustrate this in terms of both volume and quality of immigration.

13. See Eric Williams' *Capitalism and Slavery*, chapters 3 and 5, for a good discussion of the Triangular Trade.

14. It takes approximately two, four and six years of post-secondary education and training in the Caribbean to produce a journeyman, technician or higher technician respectively.

15. Frantz Fanon, *The Wretched of the Earth*.

16. From Macmillan's poem quoted at the beginning of Chapter 1.

17. For a general discussion of the conditions leading up to these riots see Sheila Patterson's *Dark Strangers*. Bloomington, Indiana University Press, 1964.

18. See "Commonwealth Immigrants Act," 1962 and 1968, Her Majesty's Stationery Office (HMSO, London, England, 1970).

19. A number of scholarly sources, including Owen Jefferson, George Beckford and Hillary Beckles, have pointed to a pronounced preference among Caribbean consumers for perishable commodities and final products imported from abroad. It would not be far-fetched to contend that the final exercise of a preference felt on such a scale by the consumer would be to remove himself or herself—to emigrate— as a 'final commodity' to foreign climes where the colonized's dream of embodying the expatriate colonizer is finally fulfilled. Perhaps involved here, too, is another dimension of Wilson Head's Caribbean man "seeking for adventure."

20. See Freda Hawkins, *Canada and Immigration*, McGill-Queens, 1972.

21. Canada, House of Commons Debates, Vol. 3, 1947, pp. 2644-2647.

22. Freda Hawkins, *op. cit.* See interesting discussion in Chapter 5.

23. For an exposition on the new selection criteria, the points system, see Appendix 1(a).

24. Freda Hawkins, *op. cit.*, Chapter 5.

25. The Hon. Jean Marchand, Minister of Manpower and Immigration, "White Paper on Immigration," October 1966.

26. "Economic and Social Impact of Immigration." A Research Report prepared for the Economic Council of Canada, 1991, p. 15.

27. Economic Council of Canada, 1975, p. 8.
28. Hon. Robert Andras, Minister of Manpower and Immigration. House of Commons, September 17, 1973.
29. "Economic and Social Impact of Immigration." *Op. cit.*, p. 15.
30. For an account of the quality of race relations in this period, and in particular the hatred that developed indiscriminately against newcomers of East Indian ethno-cultural origin, see Walter Pitman, "Report on Race Relations in Metropolitan Toronto." Metropolitan Toronto Council, 1978.
31. See Table 1(a) of Chapter 4.
32. Interviews with immigration officers at some of the Caribbean offices (Port-of-Spain, Trinidad; Bridgetown, Barbados; and Georgetown, Guyana) in the summer of 1991 indicated that the problem is often accentuated by complicated family and kinship relations among some Caribbean ethno-cultural groups. Officers claim that often, also, these complications are occasioned by marital and adoption practices of convenience. This, in turn, can often lead to considerable delays in processing the files of some applicants.
33. See David Foot, "Population, Aging and Immigration Policy in Canada: Implications and Prescriptions." Population Working Paper No. 1., Employment and Immigration Canada, Ottawa, August 1986.
34. Neil Swan, "Economic and Social Impacts of Immigration." Research Report prepared for the Economic Council of Canada, 1971, pp. 18-19.
35. See Appendix 1(a).
36. See Table 1(a) in Part 2.
37. See Immigration Statistics for the period 1986 to 1989.
38. See Table 1(a) in Part 2.
39. W.G. Robinson, "Illegal Migrants in Canada." Report to the Hon. Lloyd Axworthy, Minister of Employment and Immigration, Ottawa, 1983. Ch. 2, pp. 27ff.
40. Economic Council of Canada, 1991, *op. cit.*, p. 96.
41. *Ibid.*, p. 97.
42. *Ibid.*, p. 102.
43. Manpower and Immigration, "Three Years in Canada." First Report of

the Longitudinal Survey in the Economic and Social Adaptation of Immigrants, Ottawa, 1974.

44. *Ibid.*, p. 6.
45. *Ibid.*, p. 11.
46. For example, some workers in quest of their first jobs on arrival are still being confronted with such ethno-centric stereotypes as, "Have you any Canadian experience?" or "You're over-qualified for the job."
47. Employment and Immigration Canada, "Backgrounders to the Annual Report to Parliament." Immigration Plan for 1991-1995. Ottawa, 1991, p. 3.
48. *Ibid.*

PART 2

SOCIO-DEMOGRAPHIC CHARACTERISTICS AND THEIR POLICY IMPLICATIONS

CHAPTER 4

VOLUME, COUNTRIES OF ORIGIN AND PROVINCIAL DESTINATION

In the post-war years, 1946 to 1966, the number of Caribbean-born immigrants entering Canada is given as 29,979.[1] This volume is equivalent to 1.1 percent of total immigration into Canada during these years. Table 1 presents the picture as it was in the single year 1966. That year, 3.935 Caribbean-born immigrants entered Canada that year, a mere 2 percent of total Canadian immigration. But far more important than volume or proportion is what is revealed about the age and sex distribution of this immigrant population. The figures and percentages in the table reveal an unusual age profile. Less than 7 percent are below school age, 19 percent are of school age, 0.5 percent are senior citizens and 73.6 percent of the immigrants are of workforce age. The imbalance in the sex distribution is no less evident. Overall, females outnumber males by a proportion of 56 to 44. A similar disproportion, though reversed among pre-schoolers, shows up among the age groups 0-4, 5-19, and 20-64; whilst among the over 65s there are six women to every man.

Clearly, these distortions reflect the nature and impact of Canadian immigration policy at that stage of its emergence. Earlier, we identified the 1955 Canadian-Caribbean agreement for the supply of domestic labourers as the beginning of systematic Caribbean immigration to Canada. Both the sex imbalance and the preponderance of immigrants in the 20-64 age bracket would be largely the result of the Domestic Workers Program.[2] Domestic workers had to be female, unmarried and without dependants. The 1962 amelioration of the discriminatory situation in relation to "preferred nationalities" would have given access, as unsponsored immigrants, to Caribbeans with the appropriate "education, training, skills and other special

Table 1

Volume and Pattern of Caribbean Immigration, 1966

	0-4 Years	5-19 Years	20-64 Years	65 Years	Total
Male	146 (56.4)	346 (45.5)	122 (42.2)	3 (14.3)	1,718 (43.7)
Female	113 (43.6)	414 (54.5)	1,672 (57.8)	18 (85.7)	2,217 (56.3)
Total	259 (6.6)	760 (19.3)	2,895 (73.6)	21 (0.5)	3,935 (100)

Source: Table compiled from *Immigration Statistics*, Department of Manpower and Immigration, Ottawa, 1966.

qualifications." But it would not have extended to them the "full range of sponsorable relations"[3] which would have satisfied the principle of family reunion and preserved the age, sex and family balance in annual immigration flows. What Table 1 reveals, therefore, is that Canadian immigration policy up to 1966 discriminated towards its own perceived need for specified labour force requirements and against the considerations of family togetherness or reunion for Caribbean immigrants. Subsequent changes in immigration policy have alleviated, but have not yet been able to remove or fully redress, the damaging consequences of this choice for the adjustment of Caribbean ethnics in Canadian society.

The policy improvements of 1966/67 had an immediate effect on the volume of Caribbean immigration. Subsequent developments made the effect on volume and proportion even more dramatic. But, as will become evident later, the impact on sex and age distribution and the overall demographic balance of the annual flows showed little immediate improvement. Table 1(a) shows the picture of immigration flows from 1967 to 1989, the last year for which *Immigration Statistics* is currently available.[4] Over the period, Caribbean immigration to Canada was completely transformed in terms of volume and percentage of the national total.

During the period 1947 to 1966, Caribbean immigration had accounted for just under 30,000 or 1.1 percent of total Canadian immigration, but between 1967 and 1989, 301,361 landed immigrants from the Caribbean entered Canada,

Table 1(a)
Caribbean Immigrant Inflows into Canada, 1967-1989*

Year	Total Canadian Immigration	Caribbean Inflow	Percentage
1967	222,876	8,403	3.8
1968	183,974	7,533	4.1
1969	161,531	12,003	7.4
1970	147,713	11,932	8.4
1971	121,900	10,843	8.9
1972	122,006	8,233 +	6.7
1973	184,200	24,404	13.2
1974	218,465	27,915	12.8
1975	187,881	22,367	11.9
1976	149,429	18,172	12.2
1977	114,914	14,383	12.5
1978	86,313	10,581	12.3
1979	112,096	8,839	7.9
1980	143,117	9,639	6.7
1981	128,618	11,470	8.9
1982	121,147	11,855	9.8
1983	89,177	9,982	11.2
1984	88,239	7,571	8.6
1985	84,302	8,479	10.1
1986	99,219	12,820	13.0
1987	152,098	17,445	11.5
1988	161,929	12,393	7.7
1989	189,956	14,099	7.4
TOTAL	3,271,100	301,361	9.2

See Figure 1: Bar Chart of Above Data.

*The preliminary figures for 1990 indicate an even further drop in immigration from the Caribbean. While total immigration numbers had risen to 212,166, the Caribbean share of that number was 14,420, a percentage of 6.8. As a result, Caribbean percentage for the 25-year period 1966-1990 has dropped to 9.1 from 9.2.

+This figure does not include the cohort from Guyana, which was not available for that year.

N.B. The source of this and subsequent tables is the annual *Immigration Statistics*, Ministry of Supply and Services, Ottawa.

accounting for 9.2 percent of Canadian overall immigration. A better grasp of this overall picture is provided if we examine the period in sections: two six-year periods from 1967 to 1978, and a ten-year period from 1979 to 1989. It is important to remember that during the entire period (1967-1989), though with some changes here and there, a universal nine-factor selection formula known as the points system, is in application.

For the first six years after 1967 Caribbean immigration into Canada averaged 9,824 per annum, with 1969 and 1970 being peak years at approximately 12,000. This average is an increase of 150 percent over the figure of 3,935 for 1966. Over the same period, the Caribbean share of total Canadian immigration reveals the situation in an even more striking manner. Caribbean immigration averaged 6.7 percent of total Canadian immigration; that is to say, it is 3.4 times what it was in 1966. Another striking feature of these first six years after 1967 is that there was a progressive decline in the volume of national immigration. It was 222,876 in 1967 and 122,006, or a little more than 50 percent, in 1972. But the Caribbean percentage of that immigrant population during that period had almost doubled at 6.7. Indeed, had the figures for Guyana been available for that year, the total would have more than likely doubled.[5]

The six years after 1972 show some even more staggering increases in the volume and proportion of Caribbean immigration. National figures continue a pattern of decline after 1973 and 1974, but the volume from the Caribbean is at its highest in 1973, 1974 and 1975 with an average of nearly 20,000 per annum over the six years to 1978. More striking still, the corresponding percentage of national immigration reflected by these figures almost doubles at 12.5 percent. Even when it is assumed that Caribbean immigrants were qualifying on the basis of universally applied criteria, it should not be overlooked that the category of "nominated relatives" was heavily used by immigrants from the Caribbean to compensate for or redress the lopsided age and sex patterns of earlier years, when the "domestic scheme" never allowed for other members of the immigrant's family to accompany them. It was this staggered or serial pattern of arrival that distorted the sex and age ratios shown in Table 1. Also, the high inflows for the years 1973 and 1974 must be due in large measure to the Amnesty or "adjustment of status" program of August to October 1973.[6]

The data for the 1980s show a drop in absolute numbers for both total and Caribbean immigration. But the Caribbean percentages remain high relative to those of the late 1970s, only to fall off in 1988 and 1989. In the ten-year period

Figure 1
Caribbean Proportion of Total Canadian Immigration, 1967-1989:
Percentages

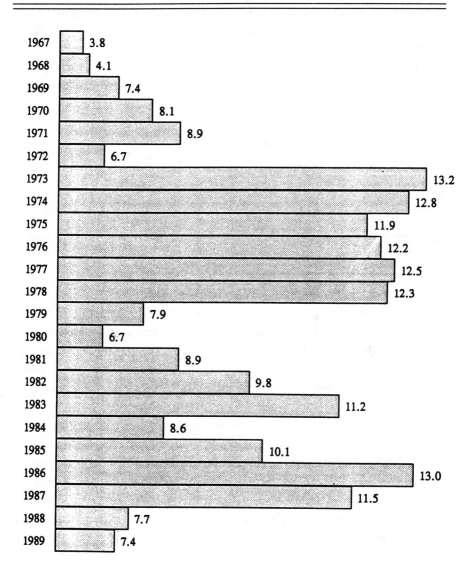

there is an average Caribbean inflow of 11,375 immigrants per annum at an average of 9.3 percent of total immigration in a situation not dissimilar to that of the first 10 years under study. It is a reasonable inference that the impact of the 1978 immigration provision regulating the conditions affecting the "nominated relatives" category is reflected in the low figures for 1979 and 1980.[7] But over the four years for 1983 to 1987 the competitive edge of Caribbean immigrants as it relates to Canadian labour force needs is restored. In the last two years of the 1980s the decline in percentage from the Caribbean reveals the new policy focus on entrepreneurs as a priority category for the expansion of Canadian economic productivity.

Despite the dynamic shifts in immigration policy over the 22-year period, what the pattern of Caribbean immigration reveals is that once the long-term and short-term selection criteria embodied in the points system were systematically applied, immigrants from Caribbean countries were meeting them and earning selection in proportions higher than was the case with immigrants from more 'traditional' sources such as northern and eastern Europe, Australia and the U.S. Over the years 1986, 1987 and 1988 Caribbean territories appear consistently among the top 10 sources of Canadian immigration. In 1989, 4 of these territories appear in the list of the top 20. Later tables will show that the Caribbean has not been a good source for entrepreneurial skills. Nevertheless it would be a fair and accurate assessment that the volume of Caribbean immigration into Canada over the period 1967-1989 and its proportion of the national total both indicate that the Caribbean area has attained and continues to maintain a "preferred area" status for supplying the priority manpower and skill needs of Canada. Ironically, as we shall see, however, this 'preference' fades at the point of entry into the workforce. The stock and flow of human capital that Canada derives from the Caribbean is disproportionately high when compared with more populated areas of the world—e.g., Asia, Africa, the United States and even some parts of Europe. Leaving aside the more obvious brain-drain implications which these data suggest, it quite extraordinarily contradictory that recent and current research information on unemployment and wages indicates that among Canadian minorities with the highest proportion of unemployment and the lowest average wages and salaries is a high percentage of people from the Caribbean.[8]

Table 2
Proportions of Landed Immigrants from Caribbean by Territory
and Country of Last Permanent Residence—Three-Year Intervals

Year	Total Caribbean	Jamaica	Guyana	Haiti	Trinidad and Tobago	Barbados	Rest of Caribbean
1974	27,915	11,286	4,030	4,857	4,802	790	2,150
		40.4	14.5	17.4	17.2	2.8	7.7
1977	14,383	6,291	2,472	2,026	1,552	634	1,408
		43.7	17.3	14.1	10.8	4.4	9.7
1980	9,639	3,161	2,278	1,633	953	354	1,260
		32.8	23.6	16.9	9.9	3.7	13.0
1983	9,836	2,423	2,605	2,827	787	250	944
		24.6	26.5	28.7	8.0	2.5	9.4
1986	12,820	4,652	3,705	1,727	940	259	1,337
		36.3	30.5	13.5	7.3	2.0	10.4
1989	14,099	3,888	3,159	2,359	3,063	309	1,311
	27.6	27.6	22.4	16.7	21.7	2.2	9.3
Total	88,692	31,701	18,449	15,429	12,097	2,596	8,410
Average	14,782	5,284	3,075	2,572	2,016	433	1,402
Percent		35.7	20.8	17.4	13.6	2.9	9.5

IMMIGRATION PROPORTIONS FROM MAJOR CARIBBEAN SOURCES

It would be considered lamentably uninformed if not an insult when referring to Canadian immigrants from Europe to call an Englishman a German or to stereotype all Europeans as Englishmen. Yet the error, the stereotype, is frequently made, in circles that one would credit with knowing better, of referring to a Barbadian as a Jamaican, or worse still, using "Jamaican" to denote anybody of Caribbean origin. At the very least, such inter-group insensitivity portrays and perpetuates intolerance.

Table 2 provides information on the major sources of Caribbean immigration into Canada using statistics referring to the "Country of Last Permanent Residence" of the immigrant for the years 1974 to 1989 and using three-year intervals. Nineteen seventy-four was the year of the highest volume of immigrants; 1977, 1986 and 1989 years of medium magnitude, and 1980 and 1983 years of low immigrant inflow. An average is struck for these years so as to provide a general picture of volume and proportion from these territorial sources. Jamaica is by far the major source, supplying approximately 36 percent of all Caribbean immigration or nearly twice the proportion of the next highest source, Guyana (21 percent). Next in magnitude are Haiti (17 percent), Trinidad and Tobago (14 percent) and Barbados (3 percent), with the rest of the Caribbean territories together supplying approximately 9 percent.

The flow from Jamaica shows a progressive decline over the early 1980s, makes a recovery by 1986 and declines again by 1989. Over the years of Jamaican decline, Guyana and Haiti make significant gains, In the case of Guyana they are progressively sustained to 1986 only to fall off by 1989. The percentage from Haiti fluctuates over the years, ending in an average (17.4), identical with its proportion in the first year of the series (1974). The trend in Trinidad follows a progressive decline over the 1970s and 1980s to achieve a steep rise by 1989 for an average of 21.7. The patterns in Barbados and the "Rest of the Caribbean" are relatively more stable, with average percentages of 2.9 and 9.5 respectively.

There must be some interesting generalizations associated with economic and political push factors that account for the variations in these territorial flow factors. Nowhere perhaps are these circumstances more evident than in the combined effect of deteriorating balance of payments problems and escalating socialist tendencies manifest in political entities such as Co-operative Socialist Guyana and Democratic Socialist Jamaica. It is here that the discussion of push-pull factors and the emergence of Canadian immigration policy, in the previous chapter, are provided with the links and ties that make for better understanding of the picture presented by the tabulated data and figures. For the moment, however, we will forgo investigating these phenomena, except to comment that it seems evident that the incidence of the brain drain in per capita terms falls heaviest on Guyana, Jamaica and Haiti; that together these territories account for nearly three-quarters of the flow of human capital from

Figure 2
Origin and Proportion of Caribbean Immigrant Inflow, 1967-1989

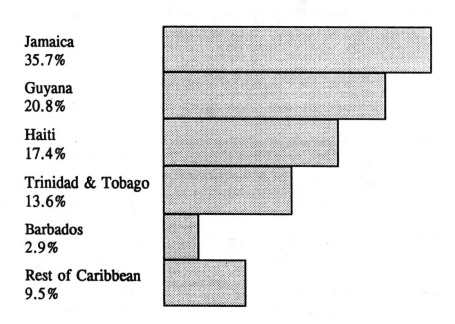

Jamaica
35.7%

Guyana
20.8%

Haiti
17.4%

Trinidad & Tobago
13.6%

Barbados
2.9%

Rest of Caribbean
9.5%

the Caribbean into Canada, and, perhaps most critically for these countries, that this marks a new phase in the export-orientation of their troubled post-colonial economy and history. It seems to be a "phase" in which human capital has become the area's chief export commodity, replacing sugar and bananas.

PROVINCIAL DESTINATION AND SETTLEMENT PATTERN

In an earlier study on Caribbean newcomers to Canada (Anderson and Grant, 1975), it was pointed out that, overwhelmingly, Caribbean immigrants showed a preference for settling in Ontario and Quebec, particularly in the larger cities and conurbations in these provinces. More recent evidence substantiates this preference. Table 3 presents the picture of provincial destination of Caribbean immigrants during the period 1974 to 1989. On an average over these years, 66.1 percent of Caribbean immigrants gave Ontario as their destination in Canada, and 25.4 percent were destined for the province

Table 3
Provincial Destination of Caribbean Immigrants, 1974-1989 (Select Years)

Year	Ontario	Quebec	Alberta	British Columbia	Manitoba	Elsewhere	Total
1974	19,210	7,129	436	540	422	268	27,915
	68.5	25.5	1.6	1.9	1.5	1.0	
1977	9,868	3,185	469	312	321	228	14,383
	68.6	22.1	3.3	2.1	2.3	1.6	
1980	6,223	2,258	521	229	277	131	9,639
	64.5	23.4	5.4	2.4	2.9	1.4	
1983	5,482	3,505	403	154	212	114	9,870
	55.5	35.5	4.1	1.6	2.1	1.2	
1986	8,907	3,001	437	136	213	126	12,820
	69.5	23.4	3.4	1.1	1.7	1.0	
1989	9,897	3,173	405	229	276	135	14,115
	70.2	22.5	2.9	1.6	2.0	.8	
Percent Average	(66.1)	(25.4)	(3.4)	(1.8)	(2.1)	(1.2)	(100)

of Quebec. Together, Ontario and Quebec accounted for 91.5 percent of these newcomers. Most of the remaining 8.5 percent was shared among Alberta, Manitoba and British Columbia, in that order, with a small 1.3 percent settling in other provinces. Up to 1976, there seemed to be an equal preference for Alberta and British Columbia. After 1977, however, Alberta moved ahead in preference while Manitoba also forged ahead of British Columbia.

Figure 2 provides a graphic representation of the sources and proportions of Caribbean immigration into Canada over the period 1967-1989. It is a pattern which, despite the temporary aberrations noted above, has remained relatively stable with Jamaica holding decidedly the lead position.

Figure 3
Origin and Destination of Caribbean-Canadian Immigration, 1967-1989

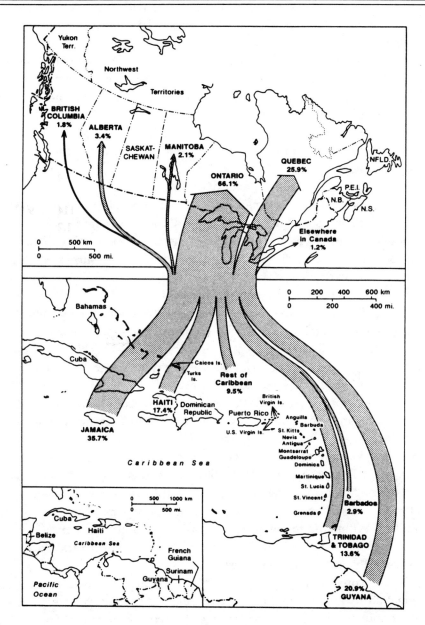

Except for the year 1983 the pattern of provincial settlement shows little variance. In that year there were nearly 11 percent fewer immigrants to Ontario than was the average over the series, with a similar percentage increase in those that were destined for Quebec. This statistic correlates with a drop in the numbers that came from Jamaica and a corresponding increase in the numbers that emigrated from Haiti in that year (See Table 1(a) above). It is evident that the interplay to be observed here between the language factor (English and French) and two major sources of Caribbean immigration, Jamaica and Haiti, did not happen by chance. But the precise explanation as to what, apart from the language factor, did actually take place to determine immigration flows to Ontario and Quebec in that year is beyond the scope of this presentation.[9]

In so far as the provinces outside of Ontario and Quebec are concerned, it is to be noted that there seemed to be little interest in Saskatchewan, the Maritime provinces and the Northern Territories. Also, until 1976, British Columbia seemed to be somewhat higher in preference over Alberta and Manitoba, but in the 1980s both Alberta and Manitoba surpassed British Columbia in importance to Caribbean immigrants.

Table 3(a) presents the percentage distribution of the 1989 inflow of Caribbean immigrants according to territories from which they came. The figures reveal no significant difference from the general pattern in the choice of provincial destination. Ninety percent of French-speaking Haitians located in Quebec. Ninety percent of Guyanese and more then 80 percent of Jamaicans, Trinidadians and Barbadians chose Ontario.

Within the provinces, the settlement pattern of Caribbean immigrants is quite regular and predictable. They continue to show a strong preference for urban over rural settings. The large metropolitan centres of Toronto, Montreal, Edmonton, Vancouver and Winnipeg, and conurbations such as the Toronto-Mississauga-Burlington-Guelph-Hamilton area, seem to provide the focal points. It is a reasonable estimate that, of the Caribbean immigrants settling in Ontario, at least 80 percent would be resident in the area from Toronto to Hamilton. Within Metropolitan Toronto itself, the largest concentrations are to be found in the boroughs of Scarborough, Toronto, North York, York and, more recently, in the Mississauga area.

Figure 3 presents a graphic portrayal of the total picture of the origin and destination of Caribbean immigrants into Canada. At a glance, we are informed that the sources of these newcomers spread across a wide range of territorial

Table 3(a)
Provincial Destination of Caribbean Immigrants, 1989
(by Country of Last Permanent Residence)

	Ontario	Quebec	Alberta	British Columbia	Manitoba	Elsewhere	Total to Canada
Jamaica	3,370	288	101	41	65	23	3,888
	(86.7)	(7.4)	(2.6)	(1.1)	(1.7)	(0.6)	(27.5)
Guyana	2,847	140	94	14	55	9	3,159
	(90.1)	(4.4)	(3.0)	(0.4)	(1.7)	(0.3)	(22.3)
Haiti	200	2,146	5	5	2	1	2,359
	(8.5)	(91.0)	(0.2)	(0.2)	(0.1)	(0.0)	(16.7)
Trinidad and Tobago	2,465	159	144	127	135	33	3,063
	(80.5)	(5.2)	(4.7)	(4.1)	(4.4)	(1.1)	(21.7)
Barbados	259	22	13	8	2	5	309
	(83.8)	(7.1)	(4.2)	(2.6)	(0.6)	(1.6)	(2.2)
Rest of Caribbean	756	418	48	34	17	64	1,337
	(56.5)	(31.2)	(3.6)	(2.5)	(1.3)	(4.8)	(9.5)
Total	9,897	3,173	405	229	276	135	14,115
	(70.2)	(22.5)	(2.9)	(1.6)	(2.0)	(0.8)	(100)

backgrounds stretching from Jamaica to Guyana and including peoples as varied as their mother tongues of English, French, Spanish, Dutch and a variety of creoles, indicate. They settle in Canada's two official linguistic areas in a ratio of 74 percent English and 26 percent French. Geographically, only 8.5 percent of them show any real attraction to provinces outside of Ontario and Quebec. The indication is that these people immigrate with a bias for settling in urban locations. According to Malcolm Cross,[10] this marks an inevitable and distinctive feature of the colonial context of their historical legacy. At the same time, it is conceivable that this transition across rural/urban social realities coupled with its geographical correlates must present a double dose of cultural shock for which supportive agencies and coping skills must provide the key for successful accommodation.

But we have moved too quickly away from the data analysis demanded by Figure 3 and Table 3(a). It should be noted that an interesting difference in the settlement pattern is provided by the grouping reported as the "Rest of the Caribbean," which includes territories such as St. Vincent, Grenada, St. Kitts and all the non-English-speaking areas except Haiti. Their settlement pattern reveals a greater degree of distribution across the provinces. Only 57 percent of them settle in Ontario, while as many as 31 percent of them go to Quebec. More exceptional still is that this group accounts for nearly 50 percent of all the immigrants from the Caribbean who settle outside of Ontario, Quebec, Alberta, Manitoba and British Columbia. In 1989, for example, there were 64 in number and represented 4.8 percent of the total Caribbean immigrant inflow.

It should not be surprising to find that these newcomers present a high degree of linguistic and occupational flexibility to the Canadian labour force. More of them for example, are likely to become involved in rural occupations (farming, fishing, logging) than the other groups within the Caribbean cohort.

On the surface, there would seem to be a clear relationship between Caribbean immigrants' settlement patterns and the linguistic skills they bring. Less obvious, but perhaps equally important for the location of these newcomers, are the educational and technical skills they bring and how these match with the location of jobs in the Canadian workforce. Much research needs to be done in this area, not merely to establish the extent of this relationship but, more important, to provide the information on the basis of which employment equity, educational and overall policies of integration at the various public decision-making levels may be devised, articulated and implemented.

ENDNOTES

1. See Immigration Statistics, 1966, Department of Manpower and Immigration, Ottawa, 1966.
2. Reference was made earlier to this special agreement between Canada and some English-speaking Caribbean governments for the provision of annual quotas of domestic workers, the first group of whom arrived in 1956.
3. Freda Hawkins, *Canada and Immigration: Public Policy and Public Concern*. Ch. 4, pp. 125-130.
4. See the first note at the bottom of Table 1(a).
5. See the second note at the bottom of Table 1(a). For some reason which, as yet, the author has not been able to have satisfactorily explained, the immigration figure from Guyana for the year 1972 is not available. But the average taken for Guyana between the years 1966 and 1971 puts the probable figure at around 8,500.
6. For the federal amnesty arrangement of 1973/1974, see Freda Hawkins, *Critical Years in Immigration*, p. 47.
7. For a discussion of the impact of this restriction of nominated relatives class, see the background paper by Shirley B. Seward and Kathryn McDade, "Immigrant Women in Canada: A Policy Perspective." *Studies in Social Policy*, Institute for Research in Public Policy, January 1988.
8. For evidence of employment/unemployment ratios, entrance difficulties and salary differences, see Raymond Breton, *Ethnic Pluralism in an Urban Setting*, 1981. See also Frances Henry's chapter entitled "Caribbean Immigration to Canada: Prejudice and Opportunity" in Barry B. Levine, *The Caribbean Exodus*. Praeger, 1987.

9.   There is an interesting piece of speculation about this that can more than bear the light of day. The period 1980-1983 was one of torrid battles between Pierre Trudeau and René Lévesque over voting composition and projections in the province of Quebec. Trudeau had won the Referendum battle for the retention of Quebec as a part of Canada, and the policies of Lévesque were driving Anglo-Quebeckers in droves from the province.

The political self-interest of the federal Liberals demanded a replacement of those lost votes in time for the next election that had to come in 1984. And Bourassa, who saw Trudeau as having saved Quebec in the Referendum, was willing to comply.

Meanwhile, in Ontario, Premier Bill Davis was perhaps thinking most about his own, calculated departure from office. He was hassled by the growing public outcry against the increasing numbers of 'Jamaican' immigrants to Toronto and its environs over the years. He was disgusted with their rapidly deteriorating record with the law. He was anxious to ease the tension within and the backlash for his own Conservative party by agreeing with alacrity to have reduced the volume of Jamaican inflows. He had been persuaded that, from a federal point of view, there could be no increase in overall immigration quotas. . . .

The answer, then? Simple! . . . Reduce the inflow of Jamaicans by the same percentage as you increase the inflow of Haitians to Quebec and let the language factor do the rest.

Thus the plausibility of the theory that the political interests of the federal incumbents on the one hand, and the Ontario and Quebec incumbents on the other, together used immigration from Jamaica and Haiti as a pawn in the game of respective political advantage.

10.   See Malcolm Cross, *Urbanization and Urban Growth in the Caribbean.* Cambridge University Press, 1979. Ch. 2, pp. 19ff.

CHAPTER 5

AGE AND SEX PROFILES
OF CARIBBEAN IMMIGRATION FLOWS

The reader must be reminded that what is being presented and discussed here is not a definitive, all-inclusive picture of the Caribbean ethno-cultural group in Canada. Both census and immigration data would be required to provide such a 'stock' picture. Only the 'flow' situation, based on annual immigration, is reviewed here. At the same time, however, it would be an error to overlook the relationship to the general characteristics of the 'stock' indicated by a 'flow' series. It is this relationship which allows one to make generalizations and to point to implications that follow from them. However, the limitations of such an exercise must be kept in mind and provide the reader with insights for further work.

Table 4 presents the sex and age distribution of Caribbean immigrant flows for selected years during the period 1967-1987. These years were chosen because they reflect the picture at the beginning, at the mid-point and towards the end of the series with which we are concerned. Over the period, females have consistently outnumbered males in Caribbean immigration flows. In 1967 the gender ratio was 43 males to 57 females. By 1980 the ratio had narrowed somewhat to 46 percent male as against 54 percent female; and by 1987 the situation had stabilized to 45:55. This gender discrepancy is not pronounced in the age groups 0-4 and 5-19. Also, it tends to lessen and normalize in the years after 1967 and into the 1980s. In the age group 20-64, however, the discrepancy stands at 11 percent in 1967, reduces to 5 percent by 1980 and climbs again to 8 percent by 1987—a quite irregular pattern indeed. Notwithstanding the relative smallness of the 65+ group, it is to be noted that among them there is a consistent pattern of approximately two females to

Figure 4(a)
Age Distribution of Caribbean Immigrant Inflow, by Sex,
in Comparison with Total Canadian Inflow, 1980

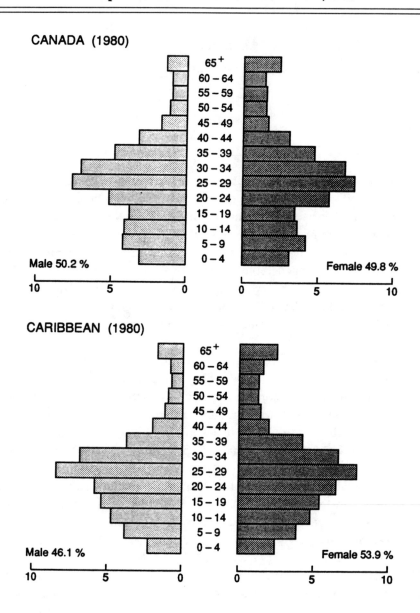

CANADA (1980)

CARIBBEAN (1980)

Figure 4(b)
Age Distribution of Caribbean Immigrant Inflow, by Sex,
in Comparison with Total Canadian Inflow, 1989

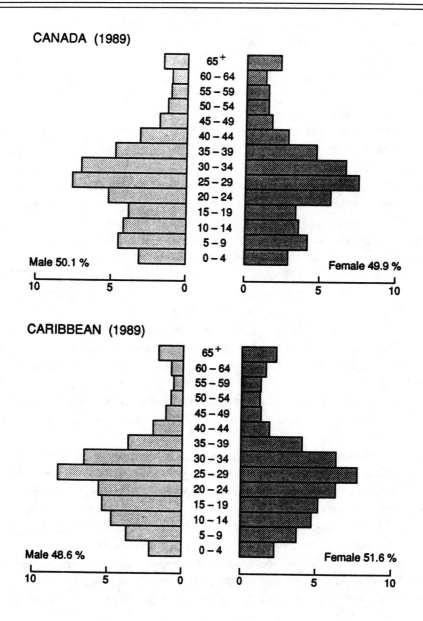

every male. More will be said of this gender disparity later on, particularly as it relates to stability in Caribbean family structure. At this stage, it is enough to observe that this gender disparity reflects the pattern of arrival[1] of Caribbean immigrants and underscores a point made earlier—that, in the emergence of Canadian immigration policy, the principle of strategic economic and labour force interests held priority over the principle of family unification.

Figures 4(a) and 4(b) provide pyramids of Caribbean age distribution, by sex, for the years 1980 and 1989 and present this information in comparison with total Canadian immigrant inflows for the respective years. The picture is clear on at least two points. First, the distribution by five-year age categories reveals that the Caribbean immigrant cohort is more skewed towards the ages below 35-39 than is the total Canadian inflow. That is to say the newcomers from the Caribbean, based on the evidence of 1980 and 1989, are generally younger, and this pattern seems to have intensified in later years. Second, whereas the total Canadian immigrant arrival picture for the two years shows a rather even gender distribution, the Caribbean picture reveals a marked disparity in the proportion of males and females in which the latter out-number the former by nearly 8 percent in 1980 and 3 percent in 1989. In other words, there has been a gender disproportion. But, unlike the pattern in earlier years, by 1989 the Caribbean gender profile was more closely approximating the balance of the total immigrant cohort. It should be noted, too, that this was happening in almost all the age categories below age 45.

The age distribution categories used in Table 4 might seem irregular. And from the point of view of five-year groupings alone, they are. Their use is justified, however, in as much as they distinguish between pre-schoolers (0-4), children of school age (5-19), people of workforce age (20-64), and senior citizens (65+ years). And these age groupings are useful for subsequent analyses.

In Table 4, the overall averages for the select years show that 3.9 percent of Caribbean immigrants were less than 5 years old; 27.6 percent fell within the 5-19 age group; 65.7 percent were between 20 and 64 years; and 2.9 percent were 65 years and over. A comparison of the age profiles by the respective cohorts (5, 17, 77, 1 percent in 1967; 4, 35, 56, 5 in 1980 and 3, 31, 63, 3 in 1987) indicates that a greater balance has been developing among the ages over the years. Figures 4(a) and 4(b) corroborate this trend. There is fluctuation but no startling change in the 0-4 group over the years. Senior citizens were just a trickle of about 1 percent in the years 1967-1974. By 1980 this trickle became a

Table 4
Age and Sex Distribution of Caribbean Immigrant Flows,
1967-1987 (Select Years)

Year	Age and Sex														
	0-4			5-19			20-64			65+			Total		
	Male	Female	Total	Male	Female	Total	Male	Female	Total	Male	Female	Total	Male	Female	Total
1967	215 (2.6)	237 (2.8)	452 (5.4)	647 (7.7)	802 (9.5)	1,449 (17.2)	2,753 (32.8)	3,680 (43.8)	6,433 (76.6)	16 (0.2)	53 (0.6)	69 (0.8)	3,631 (43.2)	4,772 (56.8)	8,403 (100)
1974	707 (2.5)	710 (2.5)	1,417 (5.0)	3,729 (13.4)	4,032 (14.4)	7,761 (27.8)	8,624 (30.9)	9,775 (35)	18,399 (65.9)	130 (0.5)	208 (0.8)	338 (1.3)	13,198 (47.3)	14,275 (52.7)	27,915 (100)
1980	182 (1.9)	205 (2.1)	387 (4.0)	1,675 (17.4)	1,725 (17.9)	3,400 (35.3)	2,438 (25.3)	2,957 (30.7)	5,395 (56.0)	164 (1.7)	293 (3.0)	457 (4.7)	4,459 (46.3)	5,180 (53.7)	9,639 (100)
1986	145 (1.1)	162 (1.3)	307 (2.4)	1,703 (13.3)	1,737 (13.5)	3,440 (26.8)	3,373 (26.3)	5,158 (40.2)	8,531 (66.5)	205 (1.6)	321 (2.5)	526 (4.1)	5,435 (42.4)	7,385 (57.6)	12,820 (100)
1987	212 (1.2)	227 (1.3)	439 (2.5)	2,689 (15.3)	2,758 (15.7)	5,447 (31.2)	4,805 (27.5)	6,152 (35.3)	10,957 (62.8)	227 (1.3)	375 (2.1)	602 (3.4)	7,933 (45.3)	9,512 (54.6)	17,445 (100)
Average Percentages	1.9	2.0	3.9	13.4	14.2	27.6	28.7	37.0	65.7	1.1	1.8	2.9	44.9	55.1	100

sizeable group at about 5 percent of the annual flow. In 1987 the process seemed to have stabilized, with 3.4 percent of the annual cohort being senior citizens.

The most interesting changes are registered by the 5-19 and the 20-64 age groups. In the former case, the proportion more than doubles from 17.2 percent in 1967 to 35.3 percent in 1980, declining to 31.2 percent in 1987. The age cohort 20-64, in turn, registers a progressive decline from 76.6 percent in 1967 to 56 percent in 1980 with an upturn to nearly 63 percent in 1987. Obvious generalizations that follow from these statistical observations would include a high visibility of Caribbean students in the school system and an increasing dependency ratio[2] within the ethno-cultural group. In addition, two sets of inter-comparisons among these age groups are significant. First, there is the comparison between the 0-4 (pre-school) category and the 65+ (senior citizens). Where the former declines, the latter increases proportionately, to become almost of similar magnitude. Thus, by 1980 the community services needed by the ethno-cultural group would have included services for the elderly. By 1987, social services for both the young and the elderly had become quite an urgent need. But institutions within the ethno-cultural group responded with only a tepid effort.[3]

The second set of inter-comparisons between these age groups provides some even more startling generalizations and implications. The figures in the 5-19 age group reveal a lag in the pattern of arrival of young people of school age to join their parents in Canada. The escalating proportion of the annual flow accounted for by this group (17.2 percent in 1967 to 35.3 percent in 1980 and 31.2 percent in 1987) could only mean that the immigration category of "sponsored dependants" was used over these years by Caribbean mothers and fathers to enable their offspring whom they had left behind when they emigrated to join them in Canada. Because this is the school-age category, the impact on these newcomers would be felt most strongly in the homes and in the school system. The culture shock the individuals would experience would include the critical stages of formative and peer re-socialization. Also, the impact of these newcomers on the education system itself could not be under-estimated. Complementary evidence from school boards and individual schools in relation to the changing ethnic distribution in their school and classroom population over the 1970s and 1980s and the difficulties that this has caused support this generalization.[4]

The percentage increases in persons of school age over the period seem to result in corresponding percentage decreases in the workforce age group. It shows that more than three-quarters (76.6 percent) of the immigrants in 1967 were eligible to enter the workforce. In 1980 and 1987 the corresponding percentages are 56 and 62.8. Meanwhile a potential school population which is 17.2 percent of the flow in 1967 doubles to 35.3 in 1980 and stands at 31.2 percent in 1987. This inter-relationship between the school-age group and that of workforce age is critical, both in terms of the imbalance in the annual flows it reflects, and even more so for the considerations of structural integration of this ethno-cultural group into the institutions of school and work.[5] The imbalance in these two age groups, evident throughout the period, though significantly improving by 1987, aggravates the difficulties inherent in the adjustment process within the group itself as well as into the mainstream society.

From the above discussion of age and sex distribution it becomes obvious that the Caribbean immigrant flows into Canada have been unbalanced both in age and gender. While the figures in the later years of the period point to an improving situation, the social adjustmental damage done by this imbalance should not be under-estimated. In fact, in some areas (e.g., dependency ratios, family life and the schooling process), the damage may already have become irreparable.

For comparison purposes and by way of identifying what a more balanced ethno-cultural age profile among newly arriving immigrants might look like for any one year, the data for three other countries are tabulated alongside that of the Caribbean.

The chosen year is 1980 and the picture is given in Table 4(a). As one of the oldest immigrant groups, it may be assumed that newcomers from Britain might most closely approximate the standard age profile. Italy was chosen because of its size as an ethno-cultural group in the Metropolitan Toronto area. India was selected because, like the Caribbean, it is among the more recent newcomers. Also, its immigrant flow for that year is approximately the size of that from the Caribbean.

If the assumption that the immigrant flow from Britain most closely approximates the expected standard holds, and if 1980 is a typical year, then the 0-4 group should contribute about 9 percent of the flow and the remaining age groups about 23 percent, 61 percent and 7 percent respectively. Table 4(a) shows that for the Caribbean the 0-4 group is less than 50 percent of what it

Table 4(a)
Age Distribution of Caribbean Immigrants in Comparison
with Other Immigrant Groups, 1980 (by Country of Birth)

Country	No. of Immigrants	0-4 Yrs.	5-19 Yrs.	20-64 Yrs.	65+
Caribbean	9,639	387	3,400	5,395	457
		(4.0)	(35.3)	(56.0)	(4.7)
Britain	16,445	1,498	3,765	9,973	1,209
		(9.1)	(22.9)	(60.6)	(7.4)
Italy	1,873	66	305	1,156	346
		(3.5)	(16.3)	(61.7)	(18.5)
India	9,531	96	1,929	6,699	807
		(1.0)	(20.2)	(70.3)	(8.5)

might be; the 20-64 group about 90 percent of; and the 65+ group just about 50 percent of what it might be. It must be noted, also, that the total volume of Caribbean immigrants that year is less than 60 percent that of Britain. Yet its school-age population is 90 percent that of Britain. In comparing this age group with those of Italy and India, the degree of incongruity in both volume and proportion is startling. Twenty percent of India's immigrant flow that year (1,929) are of school age, while 16 percent of the Italian flow (305) falls into that category. What this means in practical terms for the school population is that in 1980, new entrants to it would have been made from the Caribbean, Britain, Italy and India in the ratio of 35:23:16:20. That is to say, that for every 35 Caribbean students there would have been 23 British, 16 Italians and 20 East Indians.

Even if 1980 is in some measure an atypical year, and even when the distinction is properly made between school population stock and flow, not much imagination is required to estimate the challenge such a situation poses for teacher education, classroom management and concomitant sociological and psychological changes in the school environment.[6]

Table 4(b)
Age Distribution of Caribbean Immigrant Inflows in Comparison with Other Immigrant Groups, 1980, 1987

Age Groups	Caribbean	Britain	India	Hong Kong
1980				
0-4	391	1,515	96	236
	(4.0)	(8.3)	(1.0)	(3.7)
5-19	3,411	3,922	1,875	1,181
	(35.2)	(21.5)	(22.2)	(18.7)
20-64	5,416	11,588	5,772	4,513
	(56.0)	(63.5)	(68.0)	(71.5)
65+	460	1,220	739	379
	(4.8)	(6.7)	(8.7)	(6.0)
Total	9,678	18,245	8,483	6,309
1987				
0-4	439	563	196	867
	(2.5)	(7.4)	(1.8)	(6.8)
5-19	5,447	1,576	1,831	3,407
	(31.2)	(20.6)	(17.2)	(27.0)
20-64	10,957	4,742	7,788	8,273
	(62.8)	(62.0)	(73.2)	(65.6)
65+	602	769	820	71
	(3.4)	(10.1)	(7.7)	(0.6)
Total	17,445	7,650	10,635	12,618

In the workforce age group (20-64) the statistics, though not as startling, are quite informative. In comparison with the British, the Caribbean workforce base is smaller than it might be by about 5 percent. In fact, at 56 percent, it is the smallest among the select territories, showing the strongest dissimilarity with India. This smallness of workforce base has deep ethno-cultural and economic implications. It means, for example, that in comparison with Britain, Italy and India, the Caribbean group in that year would have a higher percentage of its immigrant flow dependent on a smaller percentage of employable workers. Based on the figures in Table 4(a) the respective dependency ratios would read as follows:

Caribbean	44:56	=	.78
Britain	39:61	=	.64
Italy	38:62	=	.61
India	30:70	=	.43

When it is realized that in comparison with the other groups the Caribbeans are wage and salary earners principally, with little diversification in terms of a strong business and economic infrastructure, this high dependency ratio must potentially be seen as an obstacle to rapid economic and cultural integration into Canadian society.[7] Stronger evidence for this point is provided in Table 4(b). In it, the data for 1987 are juxtaposed against those of 1980. For both years (1980 and 1987), immigrant groups from Hong Kong are used to replace those from Italy. In both years, the Caribbean sends a higher percentage of its immigrant cohort to the school system and, except in the case of Britain in 1987 (62.0 percent), has the lowest percentage of immigrants destined for the workforce. From this it might be argued that the cost to the public for educating Caribbean children in the 1980 and 1987 cohorts, for those young and subsequently, is higher than for the other groups under examination. Alternately, a closer look at the table would indicate that pre-schoolers and senior citizens together over both years account for 14.7, 32.5, 19.2 and 17.1 percent respectively of the cohorts from the Caribbean, Britain, India and Hong Kong. It would be both informative and interesting to find out whether the additional recurrent costs for welfare and health services sustained by the public on behalf of the non-school parts of the cohorts from Britain, India and Hong Kong are more than those sustained in relation to the large pre-school Caribbean percentages. In short, do the social services cosst for the one offset the educational costs of the other?

Table 4(c)
Pre-School-Age and Senior Citizen Population Percentages Compared
with School-Age and Workforce Percentages, 1980, 1987
(Caribbean, Britain, India and Hong Kong)

	Caribbean	Britain	India	Hong Kong
1980				
(0-4)+(65+)	8.8	15.0	9.7	9.7
(5-19)+(20-64)	91.2	85.0	90.3	90.3
1987				
(0-4)+(65+)	5.9	17.5	9.5	7.4
(5-19)+(20-64)	94.1	82.5	90.5	92.6
Average				
(0-4)+(65+)	7.4	16.3	9.6	8.6
(5-19)+(20-64)	92.6	83.7	90.4	91.4

In Table 4(c) the percentages of pre-school and senior citizen populations are grouped together and shown in comparison with those of school and workforce ages taken together. And these sub-totals for the Caribbean, Britain, India and Hong Kong are compared. In both years, as well as on average, the Caribbean potential for trainable and productive human capital is highest. Potentially, this marks a situation in which, over the next generation at least, the Caribbean-Canadians are likely to be making a greater contribution to the stock of trainable Canadian human resources than the other comparison groups.

FURTHER IMPLICATIONS OF CARIBBEAN AGE AND SEX PROFILES

The previous section discussed the sex and age characteristics of Caribbean immigrant flows. It was pointed out that the discrepancy in the gender proportions would hold potentially serious consequences for the process of socio-cultural adjustment, particularly to the extent that family dislocations resulted from the actual pattern of immigrant arrival. The disproportion in the age profile showed up most critically in the school-age category and that of potential labour force entrants. Some resultant difficulties for the school system and the world of work were observed. In the case of the former, it was the escalating numerical strength of the Caribbean ethno-cultural presence in the classroom. In the latter case, we sketched the almost circular relationship between narrow occupational base, high dependency ratios, barrier to structural integration and high unemployment levels. Tables 5 and 6 serve a double function. First, they help to summarize much of this earlier discussion, and second, they provide a basis for the continuation of the analysis of the age-profile factor as it affects workforce and related considerations. Table 5 looks at the changing age composition of annual Caribbean immigration flows under the same age categories as used in Tables 4(a) and 4(b)—0-4, 5-19, 20-64 and 65+ years—viewing these categories in selected years over the period 1967 to 1987. Table 6 draws this information into a focus on dependency ratios. Tables 7 through 8(a) take a closer look at gender proportions in the school-age and workforce populations.

Over the years covered by Table 5, the pre-school contingent fluctuates, then tapers, within a range of 6.1 and 2.4 percent. This percentage and its movement over the years are not particularly alarming. Nevertheless, the need to pay attention, among other things, to the provision of day-care and other pre-school facilities is not one the Caribbean community can afford to neglect much longer. Nor are these considerations separate from issues involved in single-parent and child adoption situations. More applied research and action in these areas should be a first call on the community's attention.

In 1967 senior citizens formed a mere 0.8 percent of Caribbean immigration. By 1981 they had risen to 5 percent, tapering off to 3.4 by 1987. Despite the decline by 1987, what the overall increase in this category indicates is the need to set in place, on a more systematic basis, programs which would cater for the needs of the elderly. Again, the challenge to the Caribbean community to mobilize for the provision of appropriate programs and activities and the physical space for their accommodation cannot be escaped or postponed any longer. Community leaders should focus their thinking on how to mobilize financial and other resources from within the group so that the needs of both the young and the elderly can be met. At the same time, social workers and researchers within the group should become increasingly aware of the various

Table 5
Age Groupings and Dependency Ratios in Caribbean Immigrant Inflows in the 1960s, 1970s and 1980s (Select Years and Percentages)

	Total Immigration	Pre-School 0-4	School-Age 5-19	Workforce 20-64	Senior Citizens 65+	Dependency Ratio
1967	8,403	5.4	17.2	76.6	0.8	0.31
1968	7,563	5.6	20.6	72.7	1.1	0.38
1974	27,915	5.0	27.8	65.9	1.3	0.52
1975	22,367	6.1	37.1	52.5	4.3	0.90
1976	18,272	5.5	40.7	50.4	3.4	0.98
1980	9,639	4.0	35.3	56.0	4.7	0.79
1981	11,839	3.4	27.7	64.0	5.0	0.57
1986	12,820	2.4	26.8	66.6	4.1	0.50
1987	17,445	2.5	31.2	62.8	3.4	0.60

N.B. Percentages in age categories do not always add up to 100 because of rounding.

public agencies and instruments in multi-cultural Canada which can be used to promote the group's efforts to develop its institutions and its interests.

Column 3 of Table 5 serializes the pattern of escalating growth followed by relative decline of Caribbean school-age immigrant population. Comments have previously been made about the magnitude of this increase, possible reasons for it, and its possible future consequences, but re-emphasis at this stage is not out of place. One factor may well be that Caribbean immigrant families tend as a rule to be large—four or five offspring being quite usual. Another explanation may be that Caribbean immigration continues to include the backlog effect of children of school age who had been left behind by their parents who emigrated earlier.[8] The actual numbers of Caribbean immigrants of school age, in fact, dropped from their mid-1970s peak of about 7,500 to about 3,400 in 1980, and rose again to approximately 5,500 in 1987. When it is considered that about 66 percent of Caribbean immigration settles in Ontario (see Table 3(a)) and that about 70-80 percent opt for Metropolitan Toronto, one is saying that approximately 2,000 new Caribbean-Canadians would have entered elementary and secondary schools within the Metropolitan Toronto school system in the year 1980 alone, and approximately 3,000 in 1987. Note

Table 6
Dependency Ratios of Caribbean Immigrant Flows in Comparison
with Other Groups, 1967-1987

	Caribbean	Britain	India	Hong Kong
1967	0.31	0.49	0.45	N/A
1968	0.38	0.40	0.71	N/A
1980	0.79	0.69	0.47	0.40
1981	0.57	0.51	0.46	0.39
1982	0.67	0.75	0.41	0.45
1983	0.80	0.53	0.41	0.75
1984	0.68	0.44	0.38	0.75
1985	0.66	0.49	0.33	0.71
1986	0.50	0.53	0.46	0.33
1987	0.60	0.61	0.37	0.53

that these estimates are merely flow figures for 1980 and 1987 and do not take account of new entrants into the system from among those already resident in Metro. The implications for the school systems and for the Caribbean community's collaboration with them are innumerable and inescapable. To succeed in this area, both sides must stop blaming each other and establish meaningful partnerships, with action starting with the highest ranks of the Ministry of Education and authentic leaders in education from the community—Black and West Indian.

Table 5 further demonstrates that the increase in the school-age immigrant flows over the years 1967-1980 is paralleled by a decline in the working-age sector and that this pattern virtually reverses itself between 1980 and 1987. This pattern indicates the dynamic changes to which the demographic composition of the Caribbean ethno-cultural section is subject, and the concomitant adjustment challenges and stresses for both the Caribbean community and mainstream society. As shown in Table 5, in 1976 the working-age component of Caribbean immigrant flow declined to its lowest (50.4 percent). By 1980 it had risen to 56 percent, which was 14 percent lower than the corresponding component from India, 4.6 percent lower than Britain's and 5.7 percent lower than Italy's. This fact draws further attention to the question of dependency ratios—within the Caribbean group itself and in comparison with other ethno-cultural groups.[9]

Two underlying assumptions are important in the application of dependency ratios to our discussion at this stage. The first is that most immigrants in the working-age cohort actually do obtain a job on or shortly after arrival. The second is that immigrants of school age do, by and large, remain at school until they are 19. The analysis which proceeds on the basis of these assumptions cannot lay claim to 100 percent accuracy, for the simple reason that the empirical research to provide substantiation in the case of Caribbean immigrants has not yet been accomplished. It may often be the case that there is no direct correspondence between the first jobs obtained and the qualifications/skills possessed by the immigrant.[10] It may even take some months before the first job is landed, but this is quite a different matter from joining the ranks of the unemployed on a prolonged or permanent basis. Nor does part-time employment while still at high school constitute full-time participation in the workforce.

Thus, based on these assumptions, Table 6 was constructed to show the comparative position of the Caribbean, Britain, India and Hong Kong in respect to dependency ratios. In it, the dependency ratio for the Caribbean immigrant flow in 1967 was quite low at 0.31. This was good; it suggested that approximately 76 percent of the contingent would work to support 24 percent who did not. By 1980, however, this ratio had fluctuated and increased to 0.79 which meant that 56 percent would work to support 44 percent who did not. This ratio was easily the worst among the four immigrant groups used for comparison that year. While this ratio reduces to 0.60 by 1987 it still stood just about equal with Britain and several points higher than India and Hong Kong. A number of circumstances make this rather high dependency ratio of critical concern. Early in the 1980s studies by the Social Planning Council of Metropolitan Toronto[11] and others reported that the unemployment rate in Toronto is highest among Caribbean-Canadians and other visible minorities. Also, workers belonging to visible minority groups in Metropolitan Toronto earn less on average than do their white counterparts for similar jobs—males by about $2,500 per annum and females by as much as $3,500.[12] A third consideration is associated with bad economic circumstances, such as Canada is experiencing now, in which unemployment is rising and wages are depressed. Yet a fourth circumstance which makes a high dependency ratio critical for both the ethnic group and the mainstream society revolves around whether or

Table 7

Age Distribution of Caribbean Immigrants of School Age,
1974, 1980, 1987 (Percentages)

	5-9 Years	10-14 Years	15-19 Years	Total	Percent of Total Immigrants
1974	34.2	32.6	33.3	7,761	27.8
1980	19.7	34.5	45.8	3,400	35.3
1987	22.0	33.6	44.4	5,458	31.2

Table 7(a)

Gender Proportions Among Caribbean Immigrants of School Age, 1987

	5-9 Yrs. No.	Percent	10-14 Yrs. No.	Percent	15-19 Yrs. No.	Percent	Total No.	Percent
Male	592	49.2	929	50.7	1,172	48.4	2,693	49.3
Female	611	50.8	903	49.3	1,251	51.6	2,765	50.7
Total	1,203	100	1,832	100	2,423	100	5,458	100

not the group possesses an economic base and infrastructure which provides self-generated employment (which the Caribbean group does little of), or whether the workers are principally salary and wage earners (which the Caribbeans are).[13] Because of all these circumstances and conditions, the high dependency ratio which Table 6 demonstrates for Caribbean immigrant flows in the middle and later years of the series can only lead to the conclusion that tremendous obstacles to structural integration and easy adjustment are posed for this ethno-cultural group.

A closer look at school and workforce participation ratios among Caribbean immigrant inflows and their gender proportions is presented by Tables 7 through 8(a). Again, the years 1974, 1980 and 1987 are used to represent the start, mid-point and end of the series under review.

Table 7 presents a picture of the potential distribution of Caribbean newcomers across the junior, elementary and secondary grades of the Canadian school system in 1974, 1980 and 1987. In the first of those years the distribution is relatively even at a ratio of 34:33:33 across the grade levels. By 1980 a definite tendency towards the secondary school level develops and is maintained to 1987 when the ratio becomes 22:34:44. By comparison (the table does not show this), the picture with groups from Britain and India shows a reverse pattern with a tendency towards earlier grade levels. This means that the Caribbean school population for the period is likely to be older than its counterparts from other immigrant inflows. A further implication is that, into the 1990s, this inflow is likely to contribute to a relative disproportion among the cohorts of secondary school graduates.

This may be the relatively good side of the picture. A decidedly unattractive side is that these newcomers might add to the disproportion in the number of visible minority drop-outs from the school system. In either case, the challenge to the Ministry of Education as the ultimate competent authority, and the Boards of Education as dispensers of the Ministry's policies on equity and non-racist education and its supportive structures and processes, remains palpably in need of effective responses.

Table 7(a) presents a picture of gender proportions among Caribbean immigrants in 1987. Except for the slight outnumbering of females by males in the 10-14-year (junior school) group, there is nothing startling about the data. However, behind this seemingly ordinary facade lies some important information. This is a time of particular promise and challenge for the ethno-cultural group itself as it seeks to understand and to provide appropriate social institutions for its young people. Often in conversations with Caribbean youth, informally and formally, one becomes sharply aware of the troubled and troubling nature of gender relations. Usually these relations are encapsulated within the question of dating and mating relations within and outside the group. From the female viewpoint one hears the question: "But where are the boys I may date? There aren't too many of them around, and those who are are too busy chasing white girls." From the male viewpoint you get the charge that the West Indian woman "plays too hard-to-get," or that her demands are too deeply concerned with going steady or getting married.

What the table points to is that there is a good balance between males and females. What clearly is the challenge for the community group leaders is to provide programs of exposure in which our young people may be brought together on a systematic basis to get to know each other in diverse forms of social and cultural discourse and behaviours, so that dating and mating processes become more facilitative and ethno-specific. This is where the structures and processes for community identity and empowerment begin and become sustained.

As Table 7 does for the school-age population, Table 8 facilitates an examination of the age structure of Caribbean immigrants destined for the workforce. The data point to equally challenging policy implications in the process of strengthening intra-group cohesion and promoting economic and social integration. The age distribution pattern of these newcomers has been consistent over the years: the highest percentages have fallen within the 20-24 and 25-29 age brackets. In 1974 it is around 55 percent. By 1987 it is 51 percent. The overall picture suggests that, on average, a potentially younger workforce is coming from the Caribbean. That means that Caribbean immigrants are likely to be in the workforce longer. From the point of view of the human capital argument, their present and long-term future worth to the Canadian economy is indisputable.[14] By the same argument, these younger immigrants from the Caribbean are likely to prove more cost-effective for Canada than are those from sources where the age profile was skewed towards the higher groups.

Table 8(a) shows that in 1987 there continues to be a gender disproportion in the Caribbean immigrant cohorts—interesting but not alarming. The 2.2 percent margin of females over males shows a weakening in the pattern of female numerical dominance. At the moment, the writer can offer no fully satisfactory explanation for this. However, in the age group 50-64 the female dominance is a massive 30.6 percent.

Push factors in the Caribbean provide one possible explanation for this. Retirement age in the public service of the Caribbean is 55, with the possibility of early retirement at 50. Many families now arrange to have mother and children emigrate first, leaving father to work to early retirement at 50, after which he joins the family in Canada. In this way, the push effect of providing better educational opportunities for the children motivates mothers to emigrate to Canada with all or some of the children. The father remains at his job primarily to qualify for his retirement benefits, after which the pull factor becomes the need for reunification with his family. The many damaging consequences of this kind of serial immigration pattern have not yet been carefully studied.

Table 8

Age Distribution of Caribbean Immigrants of Working Age,
1974, 1980, 1987 (Percentages)

	20-24 Years	25-29 Years	30-49 Years	50-64 Years	Total	Percent of Total Immigration
1974	27.0	28.3	38.6	6.1	18,399	65.9
1980	24.8	21.1	28.2	25.9	5,395	55.9
1987	24.7	26.6	35.5	13.2	9,579	54.9

Table 8(a)

Gender Proportions Among Caribbean Immigrants of Working Age, 1987

	20-24 Years		25-29 Years		30-49 Years		50-64 Years		Total	
	No.	Percent	No.	Percent	No.	Percent	No.	Percent	No.	Percent
Male	834	47.5	1,203	51.9	1,885	49.8	334	35.7	4,356	48.9
Female	923	52.5	1,116	48.1	1,902	50.2	602	64.3	4,543	51.1
Total	1,757	100	2,319	100	3,787	100	936	100	8,899	100

Thus, for a few years to come, it is quite likely that the gender disproportion in the 50-64 group, may become even more exaggerated, only to lessen later as more male immigrants retire in the Caribbean and then join their families in Canada.

ENDNOTES

1. There is an interesting asymmetry in Canadian immigration policy which should not be overlooked. It has to do with gender proportions. Over the years of our series, from 1966 to 1990, the traditional pattern of male numerical superiority over females is maintained for immigrants from most European countries, while the reverse is the case from most Third World countries. It should be a meaningful research project to examine the degree of correlation between the presence of a "domestic workers scheme" and this under-representation of males in the volume of immigration from any one territory. Compare, for example, the situation among immigrant sources such as the Caribbean, the Philippines and Britain.

    For further discussion on this gender phenomenon see the background paper by Shirley Seward and Kathryn McDade, "Immigrant Women in Canada: A Policy Perspective." Institute for Research in Public Policy, April 1988. See also *Immigration Canada, Immigration Statistics,* 1988-1990 and later years.

2. A statistic which relates the number of people in active employment to those not in the workforce. Of course the unemployed become an important component of this in addition to pre-schoolers, those in school and those on retirement.

3. See "Towards a New Beginning." The Report and Action Plan of the Four-Level Government/African Canadian Community Working Group, Toronto, November 1992.

4. There are numerous reports and statements about this in the libraries of Boards of Education in Metro. See also Anderson and Grant, *The New Newcomers,* 1987.

5. Anderson and Grant, *op. cit.*, pp. 26-28.
6. *Ibid.*, pp. 29-37, passim.
7. It is most important that community groups such as the Black Business and Professional Association and the Caribbean and African Chamber of Commerce take careful note of this in light of some of the recommendations appearing in John Dennison *et al.*, "Towards a New Beginning." November 1992.
8. Refer to discussion on serial migration in Chapter 4.
9. See discussions following Tables 4 and 4(a) above.
10. Anderson and Grant, *op. cit.*
11. Jeffrey Reitz, *Ethnic Inequality and Segregation in Jobs.* Centre for Urban and Community Studies, May 1981.
12. Jeffrey Reitz, *op. cit.*
13. Statement by Caribbean and African Chamber of Commerce, Spring 1992.
14. See, Economic Council of Canada, Report, 1962.
    Also J.E. Cheal, Investment in Canadian Youth, 1963. See also J.W. Holland and M. Skolnik, Public Policy and Manpower Development, OISE, 1975.

CHAPTER 6

INTENDED OCCUPATIONAL DESTINATION OF CARIBBEAN-CANADIANS

The previous chapter examined age and gender distribution of Caribbean immigrant patterns and viewed some of the possible implications of this pattern for school adjustment, workforce participation, and general community cohesion. The purpose of this chapter is to give a brief picture of the intended workforce destination of these immigrant flows and to point to some related considerations and consequences. But first, a note on occupational classification systems is in order.

Canada Classification and Dictionary of Occupations (CCDO), a 1971 publication of the federal Ministry of Supply and Services provides the basis on which workers in the Canadian labour force are categorized and their skills defined. It is this standard and format which Employment and Immigration Canada uses in categorizing newly arriving landed immigrants destined for the Canadian labour force.*

On the basis of CCDO, there are 24 major occupational groups, ranging from "Entrepreneurs" to "Occupations Not Elsewhere Classified," into which immigrants destined for the labour force may be classified. In addition, each of these major groups is broken down into subsets or minor groups, with each minor group, in turn, including listings of unit or individual occupations. For example, the major group entitled "Occupations in Social Sciences and Related

---

* This document, CCDO, has now been superseded by a new publication of Employment and Immigration Canada entitled *National Occupational Classification—1993*. Ministry of Supply and Services Canada, Ottawa, 1993.

Fields" includes five minor groups: Occupations in Social Sciences; Occupations in Social Work and Related Fields; Occupations in Law and Jurisprudence; Occupations in Library, Museum and Archival Sciences; and Other Occupations in Social Sciences and Related Fields. Each of these minor groups embraces a number of unit group occupations such as economists, judges and magistrates, social workers, librarians and archivists and educational and vocational counsellors.

What this classification system indicates is that each major category subsumes a complex cluster of occupations, undoubtedly requiring differential levels of skills and expertise, and consequently different length of education and professional/vocational training. Thus, while the occupational categorizations may provide some generalized information with regard to a hierarchy of standing as occupation groups are compared with each other, it would not be accurate to categorize any major group as consisting entirely of high-level, middle-level or low-level skills. Within each cluster or major classification group it is possible to find a hierarchy of skills vertically associated or integrated (e.g., from journeyman to technician to technologist/ engineer). As a result, this would make it difficult, based on level of skills alone, to ascribe functional superiority to any one major group.

The skill components embodied in Clerical and Related Occupations as a group may not be 'superior' to those embodied in Service Occupations as a group. They may just be different. In both cases the skills embodied may be essentially but not entirely middle level. Yet neither of these groups would be assessed as ranking higher in the hierarchy than Managerial, Administrative and Related Occupations where the concentration of skills may be essentially, if not entirely, high level as opposed to middle level. The Classification and Dictionary applies more aptly to distinguishing the various composite of skills included in each occupation group and among major occupations than to the ranking of the groups based on levels of skills required to perform them. Even so, differential skill levels inherent in an occupation group cannot be ignored if calibre of contribution to the workforce is to be assessed. And the CCDO, so far, provides the best available basis for this.

In conclusion, it must be said that while it might be informative to make assessments of the calibre of the Canadian annual potential immigrant workforce, in total or in territorial sub-sets, based on the percentage contribution to high-level, middle-level and low-level skills within each occupation group, for each annual cohort a more conclusive assessment must await further

Intended Occupational Destination of Caribbean Immigrants Compared with Total Canadian Immigrant Cohort, 1980 and 1987

	1980				1987			
	National	Percent	Caribbean	Percent	National	Percent	Caribbean	Percent
Entrepreneurs	266	0.4	2	.07	2,515	3.3	46	0.5
Managerial and Related	3,065	4.8	129	4.8	5,958	7.8	231	2.5
Professional and Technical	5,032	7.9	100	3.7	5,290	6.9	196	2.1
Social Sciences and Related	498	0.8	22	0.8	899	1.2	46	0.5
Religion	425	0.7	11	0.4	467	0.6	18	0.2
Teaching and Related	1,895	3.0	42	1.5	1,776	2.3	79	0.9
Medicine and Health	2,681	4.2	83	3.1	2,753	3.6	290	3.2
Artistic, Literary and Performing Arts	1,111	1.7	44	1.6	1,184	1.5	50	0.5
Sports and Recreation	119	0.2	6	0.2	134	0.2	8	.09
Clerical and Related	7,207	11.3	497	18.3	7,554	10.1	1,090	11.9
Sales	2,476	3.9	78	2.9	3,082	4.0	236	2.6
Service	4,648	7.3	35	13.1	7,926	10.3	1,634	17.8
Farming	2,462	3.9	55	2.0	1,817	2.4	97	1.1
Fishing, Hunting and Trapping	227	0.4	0	—	208	0.3	—	—
Forestry and Logging	41	.06	0	—	22	.03	—	—
Mining Quarrying, Oil and Gas	75	0.1	5	0.2	47	.06	34	0.4
Machining and Related	2,867	4.5	103	3.8	2,429	3.2	300	3.3
Product Fabricating, Assembling and Repairing	10,383	16.3	300	11.1	8,514	11.1	1,465	16.0
Construction	2,918	4.6	148	5.5	4,195	5.5	442	4.8
Transport Equipment Operating	1,195	1.9	59	2.2	1,103	1.4	92	1.0
Material Handling and Related	447	0.7	30	1.1	1,147	1.5	283	3.1
Not Elsewhere Classified	11,722	18.4	595	21.9	15,691	20.4	2,271	24.8
Processing	1,544	2.4	31	1.1	1,535	2.0	202	2.2
Other Crafts	441	0.7	17	0.6	466	0.6	75	0.8
Total Destined to the Labour Force	63,475	100	2,712	100	76,712	100	9,155	100
Averages		4.3						11.9

97

research. Also, it is important that the reader be reminded that the analysis that follows deals specifically with a flow situation in so far as potential workforce involvement is concerned. There is as yet no research available to assess how reliable a measure "intended destination" is of actual involvement of new entry workers into preferred sectors and job areas they indicated on their immigration papers. We still do not know how many immigrant workers ever arrive at their intended occupation or job destination.

If that is one limitation, another is about generalizations that can be made about 'stock' situations based on information provided by 'flow' data. Here again it must be cautioned that while the annual flow of Caribbean workers significantly affects their presence and participation in the workforce over time, only further research can assess the true magnitude of such significance. The forthcoming analysis is therefore more indicative than definitive.

At the outset it should be said, too, that Caribbean immigration to Canada on a systematic basis may have started with the supply of domestic and other categories of semi-skilled labour, but it would be erroneous to stereotype subsequent flows from that region on that basis. As was pointed out in an earlier chapter, the universal and systematic application, since 1967, of immigration criteria based on education and training, among other factors, gave a competitive edge to immigrants entering Canada from the Caribbean. Tables 9, 9(a), 9(b), 10, 10(a), 10(b) and collectively substantiate the quantity and quality of skill potential entering the Canadian labour force from the Caribbean, using the years 1980 and 1987 as examples. Together, they make a bold statement about the high level of education embodied in Caribbean immigrants—a statement amply supported by the research of Anthony Richmond.[1]

The information provided by these tables would indicate that the application of the immigration criteria was so effectively done in the Caribbean area that the supply of skills in critical need categories contributed from this 'underdeveloped' part of the world continues to be higher in comparison with other sources of Canadian immigration with much larger populations. Also, the supply has been disproportionate in terms of both quantity and quality when compared with that from more traditionally preferred sources.[2] There are serious implications here for 'brain-drain,' 'aid and trade' and 'employment equity' analysis. We shall deal with them towards the end of this chapter.

In 1980 the Caribbean supplied 6.7 percent of Canada's total immigration. In 1987 that percentage was 11.1. Table 9 shows that the Caribbean's potential contribution to the labour force for the year 1980 was 4.3 percent and for 1987, 11.9 percent. The cluster of Tables 9, 9(a) and 9(b) provides, *inter alia*, a comparison of these immigration and workforce percentages with those of Britain, Hong Kong, India and Italy. Apart from those sections of the immigrant population aged below 5 and above 65 years, the difference between the percentage of total Canadian immigration and the percentage of total potential workforce entrants, among the countries compared, is largely explained by the respective potential school involvement ratios. In an earlier section, Table 4(a) showed that whereas 35 percent of the immigrant flow from the Caribbean in 1980 were of school age, only 23 percent from Britain and 20 percent from India were destined for school. A similar statistic explains the Hong Kong situation, while Italy's large 65+ age group balances its relatively smaller school-age percentage (16.3). But we must return to a closer examination of Table 9.

Table 9 is in two parts. The columns to the left reveal the situation for 1980; the right 1987. Both parts show the distribution of the Caribbean potential workforce by categories, revealing the intended destination of these workers. Each category is given in both numbers and percentages. Column 1 shows the total number of immigrants who gave their intended destination in the workforce as the occupational areas named in the rows. Column 2 expresses these numbers as percentages of the total potential new entrants to the workforce in 1980 (63, 745). The third column shows the contribution from the Caribbean in the respective occupation areas and the fourth column, in turn, expresses these as percentages of total potential new entrants from the Caribbean (2, 712). The right half of the table provides a similar pattern of data for the year of 1987 when the respective totals, all-Canada and the Caribbean, are 76,712 and 9,155. Thus, what is being presented are two immigrant populations of potential new entry workers by occupational/skill categories—one, the 'parent' population of potential Canadian new entry workers, and the other a sub-set of the former from the Caribbean.

The comparison between 'parent' and 'sub-set' is most interesting. The assumption will be made that the occupational and skill profile of respective cohorts of immigrants destined for the workforce in the years 1980 and 1987, as indeed for any one year, would reflect the priority occupational and skill needs of Canada. In addition this profile would be deemed to reflect the effectiveness of the administrative and selection procedures in meeting these needs through immigration. Consequently, the distribution and size of occupational intake categories in any one year would reveal changing national priorities or, more specifically, index that well-known phrase, "the absorptive capacity of the labour force."[3] Not only would a rank ordering of the largest skill categories yield information on the structure of national labour force priorities, but such a ranking would provide, as well, an index for examining the degree of similarity/dissimilarity of every 'sub-set' to the 'parent' group.[4] By using this measure in examining the tabulated data presented, one becomes quite aware of the national occupational demand distribution and the response from Caribbean sources to this demand. The cumulative skill demands and the years of schooling required for attaining them, at the same time index and measure the level of skills and competencies embodied within the respective population/sources of supply.[5]

In addition to the fact that it supplied 4.3 percent of Canada's labour force needs from immigration in 1980, and 11.9 percent in 1987, the following characteristics of the Caribbean immigrant workforce population should also be noted. There is a contribution made in each of the 24 groups into which immigrant workers are classified (with the exceptions of forestry and logging; and fishing, hunting and trapping). This alone indicates the supply of a broad range of skills. The facts that these two categories are the same for both years under review, and that they are distinctly rural occupations, provide evidence that Caribbean immigrants are mainly urban workers and urban settlers. That they tend to settle in high-density city centres is not unrelated to the occupational skills, experience and preferences they bring with them. A review of the figures in the rows and columns for 1980 reveals that in five occupational categories (clerical and related; service; mining and quarrying; construction; and material handling) the Caribbean provides a higher percentage of its aggregate cohort than does the total Canadian immigrant cohort. In three areas (managerial and related; social sciences and related; and sports and recreation) the percentages are identical. In 1987, the percentages of Caribbean workers accounted for in each of the six categories of clerical and related, service, machining and related, product fabricating and related, material handling, and processing are higher than in the corresponding national cohort. In so far as occupational groups and their composite skill complements are concerned, Table 9 shows that, at the very least, the Caribbean cohort displays a sharp competitive edge—or, in other words, shares a high index of similarity with the parent group.

Additionally, it is a reasonable conclusion that, over the years between 1980 and 1987, the distribution of skills among Caribbean immigrants has shown some tendency away from the higher level of skills (and, with that, the years of schooling required to provide them) and towards more middle-level occupations. Yet, as we will see in Table 9(a), the occupational categories with the highest concentration are the ones that are in high demand. There is a pattern discernible: where Canada's priority needs change, the Caribbean group seems to respond to them. Occupational supply response from the Caribbean follow closely on occupational demand distribution indicated by Canada

Based on the Canadian Classification and Dictionary of Occupations, Table 9(a) juxtaposes the top 10 major occupational groups into which immigrants destined to the labour force are classified in the years 1980 and 1987. It presents the Caribbean sub-sets in those years against the all-Canada totals. It must be remembered that there are 24 major groups and that each major group consists of a number of minor group clusters each of which, in turn, includes a variety of individually classified unit jobs.

The percentages associated with the top 10 groups identified in the table do not add up to 100 since there are 14 other categories not included. It is of importance, however, to note, in the first place, the strong similarity in proportions between the two groups, parent and sub-set, in both years. The top 10 categories in 1980 related as follows: 68.7 percent to 68.5 percent. In 1987 the ratio is 65.8 percent to 67.4 percent. If, for the top 10 (priority) categories, there is this high degree of correspondence in terms of overall percentage to be noted, then, perhaps, half the evidence on the issue of 'quantity and quality' is already being indicated. But further comparison does provide much stronger evidence as to the closeness of match that exists between the profile presented by the all-Canada 'parent' group, and that of its Caribbean sub-set. A very significant aspect of this comparison will be the indication given as to the occupational and skill levels desired by the Canadian labour force and those provided by respective cohorts making up the all-Canada profile. Table 9(a) shows that in both cases, the total Canadian as well as the Caribbean, the percentages provided in the cells represent each of the top 10 occupational categories in its magnitude or ratio to the total number of workers destined to the labour force. For instance, product fabricating, for both years 1980 and 1987, was the major category of workers contributed to the Canadian labour force through the process of immigration. This category accounted for 16.3 percent of all potential new entry workers in 1980 and 11.1 percent in 1987. For the same years, the highest-ranking categories of potential Caribbean workers were clerical and related (18.3) and service (17.8) percent respectively. It is interesting to note that while product fabricating is not the number one category among Caribbean immigrants in either of the two years under review, it is among the top three in both years. It ranks second at 16.0 percent in 1987, and third in 1980 at 11.1 percent. More interesting still is the fact that there is in 1980, and more so in 1987, a high correspondence between the top three occupational categories in the 'parent' population and its Caribbean sub-set. Product fabricating, clerical and related, and professional and technical are the top three categories for all Canada in 1980. For the Caribbean cohort the categories are clerical and related, service, and product fabricating. In 1987, the top three categories for both are product fabricating, service, and clerical and related, except that product fabricating and service come in reverse order.

Note also that these three 'priority' categories account for a much greater percentage of the Caribbean cohort in 1987 (45.7) than is the case with the total national cohort (31.5). Categories 4 and 5 for the national cohort in 1987 are: managerial and administrative, and professional and technical—among the highest skill levels in the entire classification. The corresponding categories for the Caribbean are construction, and machining and related—decidedly more middle level in concentration. Among the top 10 groups in both populations in the year 1980, 9 categories are common with the tenth being farming for all Canada, and transport equipment operating for the Caribbean. In 1987, managerial and administrative and professional and technical are the two categories which do not appear among the top 10 in the Caribbean cohort, while material handling and processing are the ones that do not appear in the national population.

The above discussion points, with emphases, to the high level of correlation between our two populations and must lead to the conclusion that the occupational skills provided by the Caribbean and the years of schooling required to produce them are eu-functional to the Canadian labour force needs. There is a very strong correspondence in occupational demand distribution and an overall high index of similarity. The principal difference between the 1980 and 1987 cohorts from the Caribbean is that, while the top 10 categories of the former included the high-level skill concentrations of the managerial and administrative and the professional and technical groups, as did the national population, the latter seemed to have provided a higher concentration of middle-level skills, including the 'newer' demand areas of processing and material handling. But if all this goes only as far as an

Table 9(a)
Intended Top 10 Labour Force Destinations of Caribbean Immigrants Compared with Total Canadian Immigrants, 1980 and 1987

Total Canadian				Caribbean			
1980		1987		1987		1980	
Product Fabricating	16.3	Product Fabricating	11.1	Service	17.8	Clerical and Related	18.3
Clerical and Related	11.3	Service	10.3	Product Fabricating	16.0	Services	13.1
Professional and Technical	7.9	Clerical and Related	10.1	Clerical and Related	11.9	Product Fabricating	11.1
Services	7.3	Managerial and Administrative	7.8	Construction	4.8	Construction	5.5
Managerial and Administrative	4.8	Professional and Technical	6.9	Machining and Related	3.3	Machining and Administrative	4.8
Construction	4.6	Construction	5.5	Medicine and Health	3.2	Machining and Related	3.8
Machining and Related	4.5	Sales	4.0	Material Handling	3.1	Professional and Technical	3.7
Medicine and Health	4.2	Medicine and Health	3.6	Sales	2.6	Medicine and Health	3.1
Sales	3.9	Entrepreneurs	3.3	Entrepreneurs	2.5	Sales	2.9
Farming	3.9	Machining and Related	3.2	Processing	2.2	Transport Equipment Operating	2.2
	68.7		65.8		67.4		68.5

103

examination of the internal characteristics of the cohorts can yield, a more direct and startling aspect of the comparison is revealed by returning to an earlier statistic provided in Table 9. The row at the bottom of that table indicated that whereas in 1980 the Caribbean immigrant cohort destined to the Canadian labour force represented 4.3 percent of the nation's total of potential new entry workers, by 1987, that percentage had almost tripled to 11.9. Examined from another perspective, the data reveal that in 1980 the Caribbean supplied 6.7 percent of all landed immigrants to Canada but only 4.3 percent of potential new entry workers. In 1987, the respective percentages accounted for by the Caribbean were 11.5 and 11.9. The issue is about both quantity and quality. These figures leave little doubt about the high level of functionality between Canadian labour force needs and the contribution to those needs from the Caribbean. It is to be expected that the policy analysts and policy makers in all the related ministries, at all three levels of government, would have this information, would act upon it, and would instruct the competent authorities in the public as well as the private domain to be informed by it in their implementation of employment equity and other program.

This is the kind of information as well that the public would expect the media to bring to its attention in order to inform attitudes towards immigration in general and from areas of the Third World in particular. It would do a lot as well to remove some of the uglier and more ignorant stereotypes about West Indians in the Canadian labour force.

Table 9(b) presents comparisons in which potential workforce profiles from the Caribbean and four other select territories, in 1987, are examined among themselves and against the entire national cohort that year. The four select territories are Britain, Hong Kong, India and Italy. The data indicate that, for the year 1987, the Caribbean was the only area that met all three top priority categories of occupation—product fabricating, service, and clerical and related. A higher percentage of the potential workforce from the Caribbean (45.7) was classified in these occupational/skill areas than is the case for the total potential immigrant workforce (31.5) in that year. In fact, all territories in the select group, with the exception of India, surpassed the national cumulative percentage over the top three occupational classes (31.5). But the reason for this is to be found less in their co-incidence with the national top three priority needs than in the high percentages they supplied in some other critical skill need area(s). For example, in the case of Hong Kong, 27.5 percent of the cohort are workers with managerial and administrative skills, which ranks fourth on

Table 9(b)
Calibre of Potential Immigrant Workforce from the Caribbean Compared with National Cohort and Select Territories, 1987

Canada		Caribbean		Britain		Italy		Hong Kong		India	
Product Fabricating	11.1	Services Product	17.8	Science and Engineering	14.9	Entrepreuners Product	11.1	Managerial and Administrative	27.5	Farming Product	13.4
Services Clerical and Related	10.3	Fabricating Clerical and Related	16.0	Clerical and Related	14.1	Fabricating	10.5	Chemical and Related Sciences	14.9	Fabricating	7.9
Managerial and Administrative	10.1	Managerial and Related	11.9	Services	10.6	Services	7.5	Sciences and Engineering	14.1	Services	4.4
Science and Engineering	7.8	Construction	4.8	Medicine and Health	10.4	Sales	5.0	Entrepreneurs	10.9	Machining and Related	4.3
Construction	6.9	Medicine and Health	3.3	Product Fabricating	9.7	Machining and Related	4.2	Sales	6.3	Processing	3.5
Medicine and Health	5.5	Machining and Related	3.2	Managerial and Administrative	9.6	Science and Engineering	3.6	Services Social Sciences	4.0	Transport Equipment Operating	3.5
Sales Material Handling	4.0	Material Handling	3.1	Machining and Related	6.0	Managerial and Administrative	3.3	Medicine and Health	2.8	Clerical and Related	3.1
Entrepreneurs	3.6	Sales	2.6	Sales	4.9	Religion	3.1	Product Fabricating	2.7	Science and Engineering	2.6
Machining and Related	3.3	Managerial and Administrative	2.5	Teaching	3.4	Performing Arts	2.9	Performing Arts	2.6	Managerial and Administrative	2.2
Processing	3.2	Processing	2.1	Construction	2.6	Performing Arts	2.5	Arts	1.8	Sales	2.1
Averages	**65.8**		**67.4**		**80.2**		**53.7**		**87.6**		**47.0**

the national list. For Italy, 15.5 percent of the potential workers are in construction, sixth on the national list. Only in the case of Hong Kong was there a higher concentration of potential workforce skills in respective top three categories than there was in the Caribbean cohort (56.5 percent as against 45.7 percent).[6]

But priorities indicated by percentages of the cohort (national or territorial sub-set) is one thing; calibre of skills potential is another. And although both are important to the determination of overall contribution from respective sources, it would be an error to omit a few remarks on characteristic differences among respective profiles. Managerial and administrative and science and engineering services (elsewhere referred to as professional and technical) are occupational groups of acknowledged high-level skills concentration. These groups are rank ordered fourth and fifth in the potential immigrant workforce population for 1987. However, only one of these groups, managerial and administrative, appears among the Caribbean top 10. In comparison, managerial and administrative and science and engineering are ranked first and third respectively in the cohort from Hong Kong. Undoubtedly, such evidence points to a greater concentration of high-level skills provided to the Canadian labour force by Hong Kong than by the Caribbean that year. But when the respective profiles of our select samples are extended across the top 10 categories, a fuller picture emerges. Hong Kong's cohort contains 8 of the top 10 national priority categories, accounting for 87.6 percent of its potential labour force contribution in these areas. In terms of occupational demand distribution, the Caribbean and Britain come closest to the national profile. In both cases, 9 of their top 10 occupational groups coincide with the national cohort's. Altogether, Britain's cohort provides a cumulative 80.2 percent in its top 10 groups. That is to say that the remaining 19.8 percent of Britain's contribution to the labour force that year is distributed among the remaining 14 job categories of the Canadian Dictionary of Occupations. By comparison, the Caribbean concentrates 67.4 percent of its potential skill contribution in its top 10 categories, 8 of which are coincident with the total Canadian immigrant profile. In the face of this information, the Caribbean might not be making as strong a contribution as Hong Kong or Britain with respect to years of schooling embodied in their cohorts, but it certainly is a stronger one than that made by either Italy or India. And there are additional considerations. For example, 32.6 percent of the Caribbean cohort is distributed among the remaining 14 occupational categories into which skills are classified.

Meanwhile, that figure for the all-Canada cohort is 34.2 percent. On the lower side of the scale, it is 12.4 percent for Hong Kong and 19.8 percent for Britain. On the higher side, it is 46.3 percent for Italy and 53 percent for India. This picture tends to suggest that the Caribbean profile is more balanced across all 24 occupational/skills areas, reflecting a strong resemblance to the overall Canadian profile and a higher index of similarity. We may hypothesize from these data a deep socio-cultural and educational relationship between Canada and the Caribbean as political entities or 'Children of the Empire'— one that is not shared in equal measure by other regions of Britain's former colonial world. As an additional consideration in this general regard, it must be noted that when the relative size of the host populations from which these immigrants are coming is taken into account, the per capita contribution of the Caribbean can only be adjudged as superior. Also, because of the apparent flexibility with which the Caribbean meets Canada's occupational demand distribution, the degree of exploitation of their human resources can be adjudged to be more exacting. In terms of skill levels it has been so all-inclusive and so continuous. From the point of view of economic dependency analysis, this process can be assessed as inherently exploitative. From a cost-benefit perspective, there is gain in the transaction for both the Caribbean and Canada. For the Caribbean, the gains of immediate relief from their deepening unemployment problem would seem to be outweighed by the long term losses to their critical human resource development infrastructure. For Canada, on the other hand, the long-term contribution to its human capital stock would seem to greatly exceed the social costs incurred by the nation for the initial settlement of newly arrived Caribbean-Canadians. It is the point of view of this writer that there is much here that needs re-examination in terms of developing a more all-inclusive calculus for world interdependency in general and the satisfaction of mutuality of economic and moral interests between the Caribbean and Canada in particular.

A clearer distinction needs to be made between the information provided by the clusters of tables [9, 9(a), 9(b)] and [10, 10(a), 10(b)]. The percentages given in Tables 9, 9(a) and 9(b) provide relationships within each annual immigrant cohort or contingent. The presentation classifies intended workers according to occupational categories within the particular immigrant group. It expresses these categories in percentages of the total contribution for that immigrant cohort, then compares them with the national profile of classifications for the years 1980 and 1987. In this way, several aspects of the comparison between national or 'parent' group and the territorial group or sub-set could be highlighted and was highlighted. In the Table 10 cluster, the national profile remains the same as in the Table 9 cluster. But it is against this profile, rather than within itself, that each cohort (from the Caribbean as well as from the select territories) is assessed and compared in each of the top 10 occupational categories. The percentages provided indicate what proportion of national occupational/skill needs is provided by any one immigrant group, in each category, in each year.

But, first of all, Table 10 provides the actual numbers of potential immigrant workers in each of the 24 job categories codified by the CCDO and used by Employment and Immigration. That information is given in column 1. In column 2, the corresponding percentages are shown. The Caribbean contingent, numbers and percentages of the national total in the respective categories, are given in columns 3 and 4. So "3.1" appearing in column 4, row 7, of Table 10, indicates that, potentially, the Caribbean supplied 3.1 percent of Canada's occupational/skill needs in the medicine and health category in 1980. Columns 5 and 6, 7 and 8, 9 and 10, 11 and 12, apply to similar relationships (numbers and percentages) between Canada and Britain, Canada and Italy, Canada and Hong Kong, and Canada and India, respectively, in the year 1980.

Here is an example of how to read Table 10: Looking down column 1 to row 12 in the bottom half of the table, we can say that the number of immigrant workers from all sources to Canada destined for the service occupational category in 1987 was 7,926. This number represented 10.3 percent of the 76,712 potential workers in all categories destined to the workforce. The Caribbean contributed 1,634 or 17.8 percent of this occupational category, while Britain supplied 468 or 5.9 percent and Hong Kong 326 or 4.1 percent. Similarly, reading along column 11 to row 13, we can see that 472 or 26.0 percent of the potential workers in farming, 1,817 of them altogether, accounting for 2.4 of all Canada's occupational/skill immigration needs that year, were supplied by India. Meanwhile, the Caribbean supplied 97 farmers, or 5.3 percent of the national need; Britain 54, or 3.0 percent; and Hong Kong 3 persons or 0.2 percent of the national need.

Like Table 9, Table 10 provides the opportunity for comparing the relative situations in 1980 and 1987. The data for 1987 are provided in the bottom half of the table. Total number of workers destined for the labour force is 76,712, compared with 63,745 in 1980. The respective totals and percentages for the select sub-sets are provided in the row at the bottom of the table. Perhaps the most striking feature reflected in these numbers is the dramatic drop in the labour force contribution made by Britain (from 8,975 or 14.1 percent to 4,426 or 5.8 percent). On the other side of this picture is the sharp rise in the contribution from Hong Kong (from 1,964 or 3.1 percent in 1980 to 8,060 or 10.5 percent in 1987). However, over the period, the Caribbean contribution remains solidly over 9,000 in absolute numbers for an average percentage of about 13.5. This represents the highest steady flow of skills to the Canadian labour force during the 1980s. There can be little doubt that the decline in occupational/skill supply from traditional sources—Britain in particular—correlates with the increasing flows from the Caribbean and newer sources such as Hong Kong. Equally clear, and challenging as well, are the far-reaching implications these figures hold for aid, trade and brain-drain considerations and for public policy in human resource development and utilization. But it is sufficient to point to these here so as to signal the links for a later discussion.

We must now turn to Table 10(a). This table bears a similar design to Table 9(a). Priority occupational categories for the national immigration workforce for 1980 and 1987 are juxtaposed for easy comparison. The difference is that the percentages displayed in each occupational category in Table 10(a) are in relation to the national totals in those categories, thereby indicating what proportion of the particular category of national skill needs from immigration was provided by respective select territories. In other words, the table provides information about Canada's occupational demand distribution and the response to this demand through immigration from the Caribbean and other select territories in 1980 and 1987. For all of Canada's immigrant labour force potential in 1980 and 1987, the top 10 categories are listed and the percentage each contributes to the national profile is indicated. The percentage contribution of these top 10 categories in 1980 ranges from 16.3 (product fabricating) to 3.9 (farming) for a cumulative total of 68.7 percent and an average of 6.9. In the case of the Caribbean, the range is lower and more compact. The service group at the top end accounts for 7.6 percent, while performing arts, at the bottom end, is 4.0 percent. This gives a top ten average of 5.5 percent. For Britain, the percentage contributions are much higher, ranging from 30.7 percent (mining and quarrying) to 15.3 (social science and related), for an average of 22.5 percent. There is overwhelming evidence here that, in 1980, Britain provided

Table 10 (part one)
Canadian Skill Needs Provided Through Immigration, 1980 and 1987 (Select Groups: Caribbean, Britain, Hong Kong, Italy and India)

1980	National Totals	National Percentages	Caribbean Sub-set	Caribbean Percentages	Britain Sub-set	Britain Percentages	Hong Kong Sub-set	Hong Kong Percentages	Italy Sub-set	Italy Percentages	India Sub-set	India Percentages
Entrepreneurs	266	0.4	2	0.8	12	4.5	20	7.5	20	7.5	0	0
Managerial and Related	3,065	4.8	129	4.2	670	21.9	152	5.0	27	0.8	39	1.3
Sciences and Engineering	5,032	7.9	100	2.0	1,326	26.4	225	4.5	36	0.7	96	1.9
Social Science and Related	498	0.8	22	4.4	76	15.3	10	2.0	3	0.6	4	0.8
Religion	425	0.7	11	2.6	15	3.5	5	1.2	14	3.3	8	1.9
Teaching and Related	1,895	3.0	42	2.2	36	12.5	25	1.3	10	0.5	30	1.6
Medicine and Health	2,681	4.2	83	3.1	667	14.9	70	2.6	6	0.2	48	1.7
Performing Arts	1,111	1.7	44	4.0	150	13.5	33	3.0	13	1.2	12	1.1
Sports and Recreation	119	0.2	6	5.0	25	21.0	0	0	0	0	0	0
Clerical and Related	7,207	11.3	497	6.9	1,672	23.2	373	5.2	24	0.3	113	1.6
Sales	2,476	3.9	78	3.2	400	16.2	105	4.2	23	0.4	37	1.5
Services	4,648	7.3	355	7.6	635	13.7	261	5.6	67	1.4	44	0.9
Farming	2,462	3.9	55	2.2	114	4.8	11	0.4	30	1.2	210	8.5
Fishing and Hunting	227	0.4	0	—	0	0	1	0.4	3	1.3	0	0
Forestry and Logging	41	.06	0	—	0	0	1	0.4	3	7.3	1	2.4
Mining and Quarrying	75	0.1	5	6.7	23	30.7	0	0	1	1.3	1	1.3
Machining and Related	2,867	4.5	103	3.6	795	27.7	29	1.0	53	1.8	51	1.8
Product Fabricating	10,383	16.3	300	2.9	1,005	9.7	255	2.5	101	1.0	80	0.8
Construction	2,918	4.6	148	5.1	533	18.3	32	1.1	91	3.1	20	0.7
Transport Equipment Operating	1,195	1.9	59	4.9	122	10.2	22	1.8	8	0.7	19	1.6
Material Handling	447	0.7	30	6.7	41	9.2	22	4.9	5	1.1	6	1.3
Processing	1,544	2.4	31	2.0	165	10.7	35	2.3	38	2.5	28	1.8
Crafts N.E.C.	11,722	18.4	595	5.1	202	1.7	266	2.3	158	1.3	1,438	12.3
Other Crafts	441	0.7	17	3.9	83	18.8	11	2.5	6	1.4	2	0.8
Sub-set Totals and Percentages of National Totals	63,745	100	9,677	15.2	8,975	14.1	1,964	3.1	740	3.6	2,287	3.6

Table 10 (part two)

Canadian Skill Needs Provided Through Immigration,

1980 and 1987 (Select Groups: Caribbean, Britain, Hong Kong, Italy and India)

1987	National Totals	National Percentages	Caribbean Sub-set	Caribbean Percentages	Britain Sub-set	Britain Percentages	Hong Kong Sub-set	Hong Kong Percentages	Italy Sub-set	Italy Percentages	India Sub-set	India Percentages
Entrepreneurs	2,515	3.3	46	1.8	61	2.4	882	35.1	11	0.4	37	1.5
Managerial and Related	5,958	7.8	231	3.9	424	7.1	2,221	37.3	15	0.3	76	1.3
Sciences and Engineering	5,290	6.9	196	3.7	471	8.9	1,137	21.5	16	0.3	88	1.7
Social Science and Related	899	1.2	46	5.1	59	6.6	229	25.5	4	0.1	13	1.4
Religion	467	0.6	18	3.9	18	3.9	15	3.2	14	3.0	14	3.0
Teaching and Related	1,776	2.3	79	4.4	149	8.3	164	7.5	9	0.5	30	1.7
Medicine and Health	2,753	3.6	290	10.5	459	16.7	217	7.9	9	0.3	16	0.9
Performing Arts	1,184	1.5	50	4.2	92	7.8	149	12.6	12	1.0	11	0.9
Sports and Recreation	134	0.2	8	6.0	10	7.5	1	0.7	1	0.7	0	0
Clerical and Related	7,554	10.1	1,090	14.4	624	8.3	1,198	15.9	20	0.3	108	1.4
Sales	3,082	4.0	236	7.7	215	7.0	506	16.4	24	0.8	75	2.4
Services	7,926	10.3	1,634	17.8	468	5.9	326	4.1	50	0.6	155	2.0
Farming	1,817	2.4	97	5.3	54	3.0	3	0.2	6	0.3	472	26.0
Fishing and Hunting	208	0.3	—	—	1	0.5	—	—	1	0.5	0	—
Forestry and Logging	22	.03	—	—	1	4.5	—	—	0	—	0	—
Mining and Quarrying	47	.06	4	8.5	1	2.1	—	—	0	—	0	—
Machining and Related	2,429	3.2	300	1.4	264	10.9	29	1.2	17	0.7	152	6.2
Product Fabricating	8,514	11.1	1,465	17.2	430	5.1	206	2.4	23	0.6	279	3.3
Construction	4,195	5.5	442	10.5	114	2.7	35	0.8	74	1.8	70	1.7
Transport Equipment Operating	1,103	1.4	92	8.3	49	4.4	34	3.1	8	0.7	123	1.1
Material Handling	1,147	1.5	283	24.7	10	0.9	21	1.8	7	0.6	66	5.8
Processing	1,535	2.0	202	13.2	47	3.1	20	1.3	9	0.6	123	8.0
Crafts N.E.C.	466	0.6	95	6.1	37	7.9	21	4.5	4	0.9	13	2.8
Other Crafts	5,691	20.4	2,271	14.5	368	2.3	676	4.3	116	0.7	1,593	10.1
Sub-set Totals and Percentages of National Totals	76,712	100	9,155	11.9	4,426	5.8	8,060	10.5	477	0.6	3,523	4.6

Table 10(a) (part one)
Occupational Demand Distribution from Immigration
and Response by Inflows from the Caribbean and Select Territories, 1980 and 1987

Canada		Caribbean		Britain		Hong Kong		Italy		India	
Product Fabricating	16.3	Services	7.6	Mining and Quarrying	30.7	Entrepreneurs	7.5	Entrepreneurs	7.5	Farming	8.5
Clerical and Related	11.3	Clerical and Related	6.9	Product Fabricating	27.7	Services	5.6	Forestry and Logging	7.3	Forestry and Logging	2.4
Professional and Technical	7.9	Material Handling	6.7	Professional and Technical	26.4	Clerical and Related	5.2	Religion	3.3	Professional and Technical	1.9
Services	7.3	Mining and Quarrying	6.7	Medicine and Health	24.9	Managerial and Administrative	5.0	Construction	3.1	Religion	1.9
Managerial and Related	4.8	Construction	5.1	Clerical and Related	23.2	Material Handling	4.9	Processing	2.5	Machining and Related	1.8
Construction	4.6	Sports and Recreation	5.0	Managerial and Administrative	21.9	Professional and Technical	4.5	Machining and Related	1.8	Processing	1.8
Machining and Related	4.5	Transport Equipment Operating	4.9	Sports and Recreation	21.0	Sales	4.2	Services	1.4	Medicine and Health	1.7
Medicine and Health	4.2	Social Science and Related	4.4	Construction	18.3	Performing Arts	3.0	Fishing	1.3	Teaching and Related	1.6
Sales	3.9	Managerial and Administrative	4.2	Sales	16.2	Medicine and Health	2.6	Mining	1.3	Clerical and Related	1.6
Farming	3.9	Performing Arts	4.0	Social Science and Related	15.3	Product Fabricating	2.5	Farming	1.2	Transport Equipment Operating	1.6
Average Percent of Top 10	6.9		5.5		22.5		4.5		3.1		2.5

1980

Table 10(a) (part two)

Occupational Demand Distribution from Immigration
and Response by Inflows from the Caribbean and Select Territories, 1980 and 1987

Canada	%	Caribbean	%	Britain	%	Hong Kong	%	Italy	%	India	%
Product Fabricating	11.1	Material Handling	24.7	Medicine and Health	16.7	Managerial and Administrative	37.3	Religion	3.0	Farming	26.0
Services	10.3	Services Product	20.6	Machining and Related	10.9	Entrepreneurs	35.1	Construction	1.8	Processing Machining and	8.0
Clerical and Related	9.8	Fabricating	17.2	Science and Engineering	8.9	Science and Engineering	21.5	Performing Arts	1.0	Related Material	6.2
Managerial and Administrative	7.8	Clerical and Related	14.4	Teaching and Related	8.3	Sales	16.4	Sales	0.8	Handling Product	5.8
Science and Engineering	6.9	Processing Machining and	13.2	Clerical and Related	8.3	Clerical and Related	15.9	Sports and Recreation	0.7	Fabricating	3.3
Construction	5.5	Related Medicine and	12.4	Performing Arts	7.8	Related Performing Arts	12.6	Machining and Related	0.7	Religion	3.0
Sales	4.0	Health	10.5	Sports and Recreation	7.5	Medicine and Health	7.9	Transport Equipment Operating	0.7	Sales	2.4
Medicine and Health	3.6	Construction Mining and	10.5	Managerial and Administrative	7.1	Teaching and Related	7.5	Services Product	0.6	Services Science and	2.0
Entrepreuners	3.3	Quarrying Transport Equipment	8.5	Sales	7.0	Services	4.1	Fabricating	0.6	Engineering Teaching and	1.7
Machining and Related	3.1	Operating	8.3	Social Science and Related	6.6	Religion	3.2	Processing	0.6	Related	1.7
Average Percent of Top 10	6.6		14.4		8.9		16.2		1.1		6.0

1987

the lion's share of Canada's skill needs and that, among our select territories, the Caribbean limped next behind at an average figure just less than one-fifth of Britain's.

By 1987, however, the picture had changed dramatically. The national top 10 priority areas showed little change. Entrepreneurs joined the top 10, while farming lost its priority position. The average percentage of the top 10 remained steady. But Britain's percentage contribution had plummeted to 8.9. In contrast, Hong Kong's average percentage over its top 10 categories had more than tripled to 16.2. The categories themselves had changed significantly with teaching and related and religion gaining precedence over product fabricating and material handling. Also, managerial and administrative and entrepreneurs each accounted for more than 35 percent of Canada's imported skill needs that year, and science and engineering for more than 21 percent. Meanwhile, the Caribbean had improved the calibre of its solid contribution overall. By 1987, it was supplying an average of more than 17 percent of the national need in material handling, services and product fabricating combined. In the second third of the top 10 national categories, the Caribbean contributed an average of 13.3 percent, while its average over the top 10 occupational groups more than doubled to 14.4 percent. Again the data reveal, as they did for the year 1980, that while the Caribbean's share of the immigrant population— those destined for the workforce as well as those not so destined—was all together less than 10 percent, its potential contribution to the labour force occupational and skill categories was disproportionately higher at more than 14 percent.

The top 10 occupational categories within the Caribbean cohort in 1987 supplied as much as 14.4 percent of Canada's need in the top 10 categories that year. This percentage exceeds that from Britain (8.9), outdistances that from India (6.0) and dwarfs that from Italy (1.0). Only in the case of Hong Kong, with its massive percentage contributions in the "prestige" skill demand areas of managerial and administrative, entrepreneurs, and science and engineering (professional and technical), was the Caribbean contribution surpassed.[7] Together, these statistics also provide evidence that, by 1987, sources from the Third World rather than from Europe and the First World had become the principal suppliers of Canadian occupation and skill needs via immigration.

Finally, Table 10(b) turns to a direct comparison between the parent Canadian immigrant cohort for 1987 and its Caribbean sub-set of the same year. Column 1 of the table lists the top 10 occupational groups into which

Table 10(b)
Level of Similarity Between Total Canadian Immigrant Skill Needs
and Caribbean Contribution, 1987

Top 10 Occupational/Skill Categories	Total (National) Contribution	Caribbean Contribution		Percent of National Total
Product Fabricating	8,514	1,465	(2)	17.2
Services	7,926	1,634	(1)	20.6
Clerical and Related	7,554	1,090	(3)	14.4
Managerial & Administrative	5,958	231	(9)	3.9
Professional & Technical	5,290	196	(12)	3.7
Construction	4,195	442	(4)	10.5
Sales	3,082	236	(8)	7.7
Medicine & Health	2,753	290	(6)	10.5
Entrepreneurs	2,515	46	(18)	1.8
Machining & Related	2,429	300	(5)	12.4
Totals	50,216	5,930		
Average	65.5	11.8		

immigrants destined for the workforce were classified. It is important to note the composition of this top 10 list. At the top are product fabrication, service, and clerical and related—groups usually associated with a predominance of middle-level skills. Next following are two groups, managerial and administrative, and professional and technical, more usually associated with a predominance of high-level skills. Groups 6, 7 and 10—construction, sales and machining and related, may be ones requiring a greater concentration of middle-level skills, while groups 8 and 9—medicine and health, and entrepreneurs—may be categorized as embodying more skills at the higher end of the spectrum. Columns 2 and 3 list in absolute numbers the potential job contributions made in each category by the all-Canada and the Caribbean cohorts. The numbers in brackets in the column of Caribbean contributions indicate where the particular category ranks on the Caribbean list of 24. The column to the extreme right lists the contribution made by each category as a percentage of the national intake in that category.

The national top 10 occupational groups included 50,216 potential workers, or 65.5 percent of the entire cohort of 76,712 distributed into 24 occupational categories. The Caribbean contribution to that top 10 was 5,930 potential workers or 11.8 percent. In two areas, product fabricating and services, the contribution exceeds 17 percent. In four other areas—clerical and related, machining and related, construction, and medicine and health—taken together, the average contribution is 12.0 percent. In the high-level skill areas—managerial and administrative, professional and technical, medicine and health, and entrepreneurs—the Caribbean contribution averages 5.0 percent. In the middle-level skill areas—product fabricating, service, clerical and related, construction, sales, and machining and related—the Caribbean contribution averages 13.2 percent.

Perhaps the picture of Caribbean potential occupational/skill contribution can be put even more graphically by presenting the following abstract from Table 10(b) itself:

Occupation Group	All Canada		Caribbean	
Product Fabricating	11.1	(1)	17.2	(2)
Service	10.3	(2)	20.6	(1)
Clerical and Related	10.1	(3)	14.4	(3)
Managerial and Related	7.8	(4)	3.9	(9)
Professional and Technical	6.9	(5)	3.7	(12)

The top five occupational categories include three of middle-level skill concentration and two of high-level skill concentration. The first three categories are duplicated in both sets, with the Caribbean contribution in eac, easily surpassing the national average. Assuming a rational immigration policy, this must mean that the Caribbean is an excellent source of candidates for the job opportunities Canada deems to be its priorities for the workforce. Priorities 4 and 5 of the all-Canada list are occupational categories requiring high-level skill concentrations. In these areas the Caribbean falls below the national average, contributing in each case less than 4 percent. It is noteworthy also that if categories 4 and 5 on the Caribbean instead of the all-Canada top 10 list were to be used, it would be the areas of machining and related and construction that would be included. And these are decidedly middle-level in skill concentration. The conclusion must then be that there has been, evidently, a decided shift in the occupational/skill potential contained within the cohorts that immigrated to Canada in 1980 and 1987, and that the shift has been towards middle-level skill categories. In 1980, the top five Caribbean categories included managerial and administrative, in addition to the high concentration in middle-level skill areas—service, product fabricating and clerical and related—all of which were contained in the all-Canada cohort. By 1987 the latter had changed to include professional and technical in its top five, whilst retaining the middle-level skill areas of 1980. But the Caribbean contingent reflected a drop of the managerial and administrative high-skill category and the inclusion of the machining and related category among its top five.[8]

In summary of this section, then, it is to be said that an analysis of the flow data reveals that a very highly educated human resource potential comes to Canada from the Caribbean each year. In terms of the general education base to support technical/vocational education and training as well as the tertiary education to support professions in law, medicine, the academic disciplines and managerial occupations—in all these areas and more—the Caribbean has, over the quarter of a century since the points system, progressively added to the stock of human capital in Canada. In response to Canada's occupational demand distribution and the changes in that demand over time, the Caribbean has produced a supply response that has competitively maintained a high index of similarity across the sectors and across the years. And the Caribbean has done this within the context of a post-colonial reality characterized by a dependency syndrome, economic underdevelopment and the myth of 'patterns of aid' from the developed societies.

What cannot be certain, indeed, what is quite doubtful is that the policy makers and the human resource managers, at so many levels and in so many sectors of the Canadian labour force, have successfully followed the logical response and dictates of the human capital argument. From all public accounts they would seem to have failed in promoting that process of meaningful participation of these newcomers in the enhancement of Canada's labour productivity and national production. Too many of them, for too long, are made to flounder around odd jobs of convenience, before eventually obtaining a position commensurate with their skill endowment on arrival. Regrettably, some never do. The labour force as a whole suffers from that systemic dry-rot[9] which fails to balance the judicious application of trades union collective rights with the overall responsibilities of what is productively best for the firm and for Canada.[10] The Canadian experience mystique, which for newcomers of some racial and ethnic groups never seems to go away, is merely another way of disguising a virulent dose of racism and/or cliquism.

As critical observers of federal/provincial policies and practices in immigration, we are challenged to find the good sense in the following scenario which seems in a process of constantly unfolding: First, you go through a time consuming and costly bureaucratic process to select an immigrant workforce in consonance with the occupational demand distribution for that year—at the expense of the taxpayer, of course. Then you frustrate the landed immigrant by not providing him/her a support system adequate to protect against the discriminatory and cliquish ways associated with entry into the labour force. Indeed, you are willing, again at the taxpayers' expense, to assist in the re-education of people who, as a condition for landed status in the first place, already possessed required categories of qualification and of experience but are now being deemed unacceptable for entry to their chosen occupational category. And you, the Immigration Authority, to do little to either save the burdened taxpayer or to rescue the hapless and frustrated immigrant from the process.

What, then, in the final analysis, is the value that is more regarded: the human capital potential embodied in the immigrant, or the unspoken ethic of racial and ethnic discrimination that pervades Canada and much of the so-called developed world? The depth of the cynicism is perhaps disguised in the realization that, in fact, immigrant labour is not labour whose education and training has been paid for by the host state. It is at best no better than captive labour as developed nations exercise their economic notions of comparative advantage over developing states and do so without moral scruple. And there is, as yet, no protocol by which a system of transfer payments can become due and payable to donor countries for this contribution of human resource aid. A closer look at the picture indicates other areas of inconsistencies in policy. The Canadian refugee situation is one such. Is it too outlandish to think that the tax dollars devoted to the system become like charitable donations paid to ease the nation's troubled conscience over a growing gap between the rich nations and the poor? And, if this is so, how can the policy makers still marvel at the nation's mounting cynicism towards immigration?

The implementation and monitoring of employment equity legislation as well as the vigilance of ethno-cultural groups in asserting their right to appropriate employment on arrival, and promotion subsequently, are absolutely essential to the correction of the situation presented by the above scenario. And leadership, in terms of developing the initiatives and sustaining partnerships to correct the general and their own specific situation must emanate from the Caribbean ethno-cultural community itself.

ENDNOTES

1. See Anthony Richmond, *Caribbean Immigrants: A Demo-Economic Analysis*. Statistics Canada, Ottawa, 1989.
2. This is further borne out, as indicated later, by the application of a similarity/dissimilarity index between the national inflow and the Caribbean sub-set on the one hand, and those from so-called preferred areas such as Western Europe, Australia and New Zealand.
3. See Freda Hawkins, *Canada and Immigration*, pp. 79-88, passim.
4. W. Kalbach, "Ethnic Residential Segregation and the Significance for the Individual in an Urban Setting." Centre for Urban and Community Studies, University of Toronto, 1981. See also brief discussion by Richmond *op. cit.*, Appendix B, p. 71.
5. It is quite possible, by the construction of a weighted index for secondary and tertiary education and training, to come up with a measure of years of schooling and on-the-job training invested in each skill area, and thus the immigrant sub-set as a whole. See F. Harbison and C. Myers, *Education, Manpower and Economic Growth: Strategies for Human Resource Development*. New York. McGraw Hill, 1963.
6. There can be little doubt that, whether the policy is explicitly stated or not, Canada periodically turns to appropriate sources to satisfy its overall demand for specific categories of skills and expertise. How else would one explain the 'courting,' the additional staff appointments, and the heavy inflow of the entrepreneurial category from Hong Kong over the closing years of the 1980s and the opening ones of the 1990s? It needs to be acknowledged, however, that specialization in providing a particular class or category of skills to meet specific periodical needs of the host society is not the same as providing, over the long run, a high index of similarity with its

annual occupational demand distribution.

7. Of course this is partially explained as well in the rather unusual and urgent push factor now being experienced by entrepreneurs and the highly educated in Hong Kong. In 1997, the British government hands back the territory to China.

8. Even so, there would seem to be little support here for Anthony Richmond's statement, on page 5 of his *Caribbean Immigrants*, that "The average educational level among earlier immigrants was high but was lower among those who arrived after 1974."

9. Others may prefer to call it just plain racism.

10. An interesting study on public policy and the role of trades unions, with particular relation to the NDP government's initiatives of social contract and employment equity, is indicated here.

CHAPTER 7

SUMMARY AND CONCLUSION:
SOME POLICY IMPLICATIONS

I

The discussion has presented a demographic exploration of the Caribbean ethno-cultural group in Canada based on immigration data over the past two and a half decades. The picture presented has its inherent limitations in as much as complementary census information is absent. Nevertheless, it casts light on some salient features of these newcomers which should be at the centre of the development and articulation of policy at the intra-group as well as at public institutional levels.

Since 1966, no fewer than 300,000 Caribbean immigrants have joined the Canadian mosaic. The volume and pattern of their arrival have followed the emergence of Canadian immigration policy, which has seen the removal of official, if not systemic, forms of discrimination based on ethnicity and race. The arrival pattern has been determined in part also by the skilled manpower exigencies of the Canadian labour force. It has been revealed that while Jamaica accounts for nearly 40 percent of the immigration from the Caribbean, the remaining 60 percent is composed of inflows from some 20 other territories, reflecting differences of national origin, language, religion and race, but sharing a common heritage distilled from a creolization process in which at least three civilizations have participated. Caribbean immigrants settle, in large majority, in urban centres close to the jobs for which their skills qualify them. Nearly 90 percent of them choose the provinces of Ontario and Quebec, with almost 70 percent coming to Ontario.

The arrival pattern since 1967 reveals a gender disproportion: females outnumber males significantly. But this disproportion has reduced from more than 13 percent in 1967 to 10 percent in 1980. A little less than one-third of the incoming population, on average, over the years, was younger than 20, while nearly two-thirds were between 20 and 65. By 1987, the percentage of persons 65 and over had grown from 0.8 to 3.4, while the percentage of infants, under 5 years, had fallen by more than half. There has been a massive increase in the percentage of the Caribbean immigrant group destined for the school system. In 1967 it was 17.2, in 1980 it was 35.3, and by 1987 it was 31.2. During the same period, a working-age population that was 76.6 percent of the Caribbean inflow in the years before 1980 dropped dramatically to 56 in 1980, but recovered to 62.8 by 1987.

These percentages are important for understanding the magnitude of the impact on the school system and the labour force which they suggest. For example, as far as the school system is concerned, of all visible minorities, Caribbean newcomers provide the largest proportion of their annual immigrant flows to the classrooms of Metropolitan Toronto. In the last years of the 1970s and the first year of the 1980s, the Caribbean potential school-age population had its highest percentage destined for the senior forms of public schools, a percentage which was, at the same time, higher than that of the other visible minority groups examined, except East Indians. Further, the equally large numbers destined by age for the workforce would for years be in competition for scarce jobs, particularly at the new entry worker level. The indication is that the old handicap of 'no Canadian experience' still is a compounding factor assuring the Caribbean newcomer an unenviable position among the ranks of the unemployed and under-employed. The worse the overall economic situation becomes, the higher the probability that the first-job seeker among the Caribbean ethno-cultural group, either newly arriving or recently leaving school, will become an unemployment casualty. Collaborative initiatives on the part of various levels of government, private enterprise and the ethno-cultural community in challenging and remedying this situation cannot be postponed any longer.

If most of the above information provides a picture of general trends and unsubstantiated consequences, then the need for research of a secondary, detailed and systematic nature, dealing with the many and complex aspects of the adjustment experience of Caribbean-Canadians, is patently urgent. The principal producers of such research must be Caribbean-Canadians themselves. It is not enough that this group becomes famous for its contributions to those expressive parts of Canadian culture that are colourful and sensational. The group must become more deeply engaged through dynamic participation in the public institutional life of Canadian society, in its economy, its politics, its media and its chambers of instrumental power. None of this can happen without a heightened level of self-knowledge within the group. Such knowledge is at the base of the transactional process through which increasing degrees of penetration of public institutional life can be achieved and maintained. Neither affirmative action, compensatory programs, nor tokenism, however necessary as components in a total strategy, can supply a sufficient psycho-social framework for that strategy.

Equity education, employment equity and equity participation in general are the goals to be focussed on and achieved by Caribbean-Canadians in their process of integration into Canadian society. A principal struggle for them must be towards influencing and hastening the development of equity policies and their implementation at all levels and in all sections of public life. All of this rests fundamentally on the determination of the group to place intra-group institution building at the centre of its program of empowerment. The ensuing section will deal with this in some greater detail.

To know themselves, to define themselves, to interpret the socio-political environment in terms of their own strengths and shortcomings, and then to engage in the transactional process—these are the challenges that face Caribbean-Canadians. I hope this book provides some assistance in the development of that process.

II

It would be an unfortunate shortcoming to end this text without presenting at least a brief generalized picture of some critical elements that operate to affect the process of adjustment of Caribbean newcomers to Canadian host society. A number of issues may be isolated for our attention. Major ones among them are public attitudes towards immigration and the presence of racist attitudes and behaviours in the society. In 1977, a study commissioned by the Ministry of State for Multiculturalism found:

Although there is general tolerance toward immigration, there are some indications of concern. Greater unemployment is seen as a possible consequence of further immigration. Should economic circumstances decline and concern for unemployment increase, attitudes toward immigration may well change. While a majority of Canadians show racial tolerance, there is a minority for whom race is an important concern. The admission of an increased number of non-white immigrants may mobilize the racist minority and/or increase its membership. Another sign for the concern is the inverse relationship between socio-economic status and attitudes toward immigration. The more negative attitudes toward immigration among lower status people may be reinforced to the extent that these people see immigrants as competitors for scarce jobs. This process may be accelerated by a deterioration of the economy and increased unemployment.[1]

That was in 1977. Since then, immigration from visible minority sources has increased considerably and the Caribbean has maintained its percentage of the total annual intake at 9.2. Recently, in the province of Ontario, and in Toronto in particular, the issues of racism and differential group and individual opportunities all across the society have become more striking and the calls for their correction more strident. The economic recessions of the 1980s and 1990s, in particular the latest one through which we are still struggling, have been accompanied by unprecedented levels of unemployment and social hardships. As a sequel to the Yonge Street upheaval in April 1992, when elements of the youth of Toronto, including those of Caribbean-Canadian descent, erupted in acts of riotous behaviour and vandalism, the New Democratic government responded promptly. It set up a one-man inquiry. The Stephen Lewis Committee was mandated to report to the Premier in 30 days on the causes of the behaviour and make recommendations for dealing with them. The first of four initial observations made by Mr. Lewis was:

First, what we are dealing with, at root and fundamentally, is anti-Black racism. While it is obviously true that every visible minority community experiences the indignities and wounds of systemic discrimination throughout Southern Ontario, it is the Black community which is the focus. It is Blacks who are being shot, it is Black youth that are under-employed in excessive numbers, it is Black students who are being inappropriately streamed in schools, it is Black kids who are disproportionately dropping out, it is housing communities with large concentrations of Black residents where the sense of vulnerability and disadvantage is most acute, it is Black employees, professional and non-professional, on whom the doors of upward equity slam shut. Just as the soothing balm of Multiculturalism cannot mask racism, so racism cannot mask its primary target.[2]

Though continually recounted from various perspectives at committee meetings, conferences and in numerous reports across Ontario and other provinces,[3] the picture painted here by Lewis is perhaps the most succinct, the most graphic of accounts in any one place of the settlement and adjustment in Canada of Blacks and visible minorities. And it needs to be emphasized that Caribbean-Canadians fall almost exclusively into this category. Lewis has put his finger on the critical stress points at which racism continues to undermine the good health of our multicultural body politic. Either from the point of view of a social philosophy that extols participatory democracy and the equality of opportunity that goes with it, or from the narrower utilitarian dictates of the human capital concept, this deepening pattern of difficulties of adjustment of Blacks and Caribbeans who form a substantial collectivity within that category makes no sense. It can only be assessed as blind and self-serving on the part of policy-making elites and those sections of the masses that would be described by Freire as existing in a state of "naive transitivity."[4]

The socio-demographic profile of Caribbeans given in the preceding chapters has shown that these immigrants and their ethno-cultural group are among the most highly educated newcomers[5] to Canada. They are a younger population from whom the host society can potentially expect a stream of productive benefits far in excess of the health and welfare costs to be sustained by the public fisc. At the very least, a commonsense approach to public policy would/should suggest that it might be cheaper to sustain the investment costs associated with equity participation of Black youth in school and society, thereby defusing their frustration and destructive anger, rather than incurring the inevitably delayed and direct costs of property damage, and the other social correctional costs that are the concomitants of rampages and destruction of public and private property. The cost in human lives is also a high cost to society not to be forgotten. From this theoretical perspective the practical realities and possibilities of Caribbean integration seem generally bleak.

At times, however, the critical observer feels that all is not lost that some little progress has been made along the way and that the society might well be at the turning point for the better. One such event of promise in Ontario has been the Minister of Education's direction through the House of Bill 21, an Act to amend the Education Act.[6] Principally, the Act provides for mandatory ethno-cultural equity and anti-racist educational programs across all Boards and schools, and a tightening of the focus on accountability at all levels of the system for attaining these objectives. In an act of bold initiative, the Minister has caused to be created a new Assistant Deputy Minister portfolio within the administrative structure, in the hope that this will further facilitate the Ministry's task in the change of values and attitudes among Board members, teacher educators, superintendents, principals and teachers. All these personnel must now be monitored in holding a collective responsibility for the achievement of equity and anti-racist education.

To some Caribbean-Canadians, this may appear merely a belated "opening foray into affirmative action"[7] with all the demeaning connotations associated with that term. To many others, this Bill has prepared the ground for a more meaningful partnership among the Ministry, the Boards of Education, and the Caribbean and other visible minority communities in solving one of the nation's most vexing problems. For the aforementioned Caribbean-Canadians, a mood of cynicism finds utterance in an inability to "understand why the schools have been so slow to reflect the broader society,"[8] though the deeper irony of that statement may not be lost on them. For the more serious-minded activist, the challenge for empowerment within the educational sector rests with the resoluteness of the community to create and sustain areas of meaningful partnership and dialogue with the system. Essentially, for all Caribbean-

Canadians, a sense of identity and self-esteem as an ethno-cultural group is the foundation-stone of the task. All too rarely is this understood. As a result countless attempts at establishing solidarity and self-reliance within the group have failed.

The John Brooks Community Foundation[9] recently produced a documentary with Rogers Cable, entitled *Yes, I Can*, which exemplified self-affirmation among the Caribbean-Canadians. What is particularly striking and effective about this presentation is that the young people are allowed to speak for themselves about the challenges that the system presents and about their own successes, buttressed on family and community support, in responding to those challenges. As these young people tell their stories, uninterrupted by the perspectives and biases of the 'outsider' as it were, they empower themselves. They act as genuine role models for their peers. They point to the kinds of support systems for compensatory education and teenage re-socialization that the Caribbean ethno-cultural community needs urgently to provide for its members. Thus, they become actively involved in defining themselves, defining the problems and identifying the solutions, within the context of vigilant family and community support structures.

But, as with public decision making in a plural society, particularly in the area of policy initiatives aimed at bringing about change in sensitive issues such as race relations and education, a note of caution is always in order. On this occasion it must be stated that, while the dialogue and the developing partnership between the Black community and the chief political incumbents in the Ministry of Education still goes on, one cannot be sure that the most senior civil servants of the Ministry all stand ready to exhibit that professional edge of accountability which accords, in the final analysis, full support to the public participation process. It would not be surprising, for example, if, for reasons of systemic pre-disposition, the changes envisaged by Bill 21 came to be interpreted as threatening to some senior Ontario civil servants, causing them to withhold support or to simply sabotage it. Such an eventuality would not be new. Rumblings about changes to the process, if not the principle, of appointing a new Assistant Deputy Minister to pilot anti-racist and equity education into the administrative structure of the Ministry and outwards into the Boards and schools is not at all a good omen.

A companion piece of provincial legislation to the revised Education Act, which can mean so much to Caribbean-Canadians, is Bill 79, "An Act to provide for Employment Equity for Aboriginal People, People with Disabilities,

Members of Racial Minorities and Women."[10] At the time of writing, the Bill is approaching its second reading in the House and is presenting some degree of heightened hope to disadvantaged sections of the Ontario community. But it should be cautioned that systemic discrimination based on race is not confined to the education system. Racist sentiments, attitudes and behaviours have ramifications for the entire society. Thus, employment equity, in negotiation and in practice, presents no simpler challenge in the workplace than does equity education in the schools. In fact, the difficulties in one significantly reinforce the problems in the other. For example, the school drop-out who, as a newcomer with a Caribbean heritage, has been channelled through a streaming system in an ethno-centric school environment, presents a prime target for further victimization as she or he seeks a first job or promotion in the workforce.

Thus, the response to this legislation by Caribbean-Canadians, as a sub-group falling within the designated groups of racial minorities and women, must be careful and informed.

While some employers have recently been moving more closely towards the adoption of fairer employment practices, it is government's concern that voluntary efforts alone do not adequately address the systemic discrimination that bars designated groups from equal access to entry and promotional opportunities. Hence the mandatory legislative approach. But the legislation itself means little without a reciprocal public vigilance. In other words, Bill 79, even when it becomes law, will fail to produce the optimal desired effect for Caribbean-Canadians until they themselves, as a group, can mobilize and network to bring the most powerful lobbying influence to bear in the negotiating, implementing, monitoring and evaluating stages of the exercise. Employment equity is not a magic phrase. It does not confer instant accomplishment; rather, it summons us, designated groups as well as the community at large, to a state of readiness and willingness to stand for public accountability in the workplace. The obligation of employers to conduct the labour force surveys on the basis of which the plans for employment equity implementation, appropriately time-tabled, can be designed, are important areas for the exercise of vigilance and participation by Caribbean-Canadian and other community groups. So also will this vigilance be necessary to ensure that there is compliance with the Equity Commission and its Tribunal.

There can be little doubt that this is an area for the Caribbean community in which the scope for the initiation of partnerships with public and private sectors of the workforce can be both wide and rewarding. The demographic features of the community, indicated at the immigrant inflow level in the chapters above, present but one part of a fuller data base required for informing about the education and skill composition available to the workforce from the Caribbean ethno-cultural section. Over and above that, stock and information about the changing pattern of that stock are necessary. Thus, the types of partnerships envisaged must include the development and delivery of empirical labour force research findings which will enhance the data base for employment equity implementation plans and strategies for all concerns and interests. The responsibility for the initiatives in making this possible lies, in the first place, squarely with the Caribbean-Canadian community.

One final point at this stage. Caribbean inflows to the Canadian labour force over the past 25 years have been shown to be a highly competitive source of human capital for Canada in comparison with other groups examined. It would be nothing short of criminal neglect if either the group or the society at large were to fail to adopt adequate measures conducive to the maximizing of benefits.

Another area of public life not only sensitive but critical to the integration process of Caribbean newcomers into Canadian society is that of the criminal justice system. After all, it is this system, at all its levels and in all its elements, that represents the protective core of the moral and ethical values by which Canadians live. It is the criminal justice system that must seek assiduously to review, refine and recommend on public behaviour, including its own. It must do this pursuant to the sensitivities it develops about ethno-cultural realities and cross-cultural transactions within the context of the individual's constitutional rights and freedoms. Yet, incidents of the perception and/or the practice of racism against Blacks and visible minorities in general and Caribbean-Canadians in particular have become an escalating staple of news reports on an almost daily basis. The ugly and wicked stereotypes of domestic violence and crime, "shit-disturbing" in and drop-outs from the school system have become firmly attached to Caribbean blacks. Racist perceptions have become fact in public estimation and among decision makers. And it is the media that, for the most part, portray and reinforce this image.

One sometimes gets the impression that there is a certain liberty exercised by the media in these matters which coincides with a permissiveness of response by the criminal justice system, and that that may be leading to a denial of equality of status before the law for some groups.

It would be no exaggeration to say that the criminal justice system in Ontario is not altogether free from this damaging perception. In all aspects of this complex system, shocking public indictments have been made

> from the behaviour and remarks of courtroom judges in delivery of their instructions to the jury, and in their judgement, to the crown attorneys and the plea bargaining process, and the jury selection system, to the recruitment, selection and training of police officers especially in crucial areas such as race relations and in the use of deadly force; their attitude and demeanour to suspects on the street and in the police precincts; their perception of community policing, to the Offices of the Police Complaints Commissioner and the Special Investigation Unit, to the Parole System and the Correction Officers in the Detention Centres.*

All of these, and in particular the matter of the police and policing, have been at one stage or another the targets of public criticism as to the discharge of their duties and responsibilities, and their perception of public accountability.

Over the past two decades, there has been no scarcity of treatment in the literature on matters associated with the operation of the criminal justice system in Ontario. In particular, there has been no shortage on the issue of police and minority group relations. Clare Lewis[11] has pointed out that from Carter to Gerstein, Pitman to Morand to Maloney, reports have covered all aspects of the policing issue. Equally striking in the province has been the measure of cynicism which has grown around public attitude to the criminal justice and policing systems largely because so little has been done by way of positive action on these reports.

More recently, there came the attempt of Stephen Lewis.[12] For 14 pages, nearly two-fifths of his 37-page report, he directed searching attention to the criminal justice system, graphically reporting what a wide range of public respondents had communicated to him. He set down some critical and timely

---

*   Excerpted from the Clare Lewis and the Stephen Lewis Reports at the author's discretion.

recommendations impressively crafted around previous findings and suggestions. He presented them with proposed guidelines and dates for implementation. Needless to say, most of these dates have passed without the expected action either being undertaken or completed. A flurry of committee meetings held by government offices and the Black community, separately and in conjunction have now more or less, fizzled into the customary pattern of irresolute bureaucratic shuffling.

Thus, the question must be posed bluntly. Are the intentions of the political directorate and the implementational support of the bureaucracy merely a show of good intentions towards the conventions of capitalist democracy? Are they really lacking the will or the conviction to bring about desired change? Is the NDP's drive for meaningful change in social relations in Ontario exposing and irritating the traditional sepsis between political will and bureaucratic vested interest? At another level of analysis, one may want to ask whether what is at work is not some sort of classic neo-Marxist conflict model. In such a model, the hegemonic demands of Canada's cultural dualism, traditionally revered and draped in Durkheimian garb of organic solidarity and stability, is now besieged in battle, but stubbornly refuses to make accommodation for other ethno-cultures except where a condition of abject capitulation has been perceived as a result of revolutionary violence—and, even then, only as a truce of convenience to be reneged upon the instant the crisis is over. In other words, to press the classical parallel further, there would seem to be as yet no state of readiness in which the Weberian formula of symbolic interactionism may be applied in the interest of bringing about negotiated common meaning within a multicultural democracy and on a durable and lasting basis. Or, in a more prophetic vein, are these all symptoms of the bankruptcy of capitalist democracy?

For the scholar, the general public and the young Canadian citizen of the future, the task is to understand the changing dynamics of a world that ethno-centrism has built, but which has indeed become a global village where collectivities of nationalities and ethno-cultures have become pressed into common defining technologies of mass society. The new crucibles of epistemology and appropriate structures; the media, the education and criminal justice systems; the language, the metaphors and the stereotypes; in short, the "new world order" can no longer be dominantly Euro-centric. It must include as well the Afro-centric, the Indo-centric, the Asio-centric.

Finally, as is inevitably the case for all other visible minority cultures arriving in Canada today, a challenging process of culture shock and change awaits. It is inescapable for all newcomers. None can be excluded from it, and it is futile to seek to opt out of it. Unlike most other groups, however, Caribbean newcomers have, as a people, already been the agents of change within a prior multicultural process. And their cultural antecedents, their historical past, will not desert them. It is for them, with resolve, to fully exercise and to demonstrate the expressive as well as the instrumental high points of their cultural diversity. For this is their destiny. They have passed this way before.

ENDNOTES

1. John W. Berry, R. Kalin, and D. Taylor, *Multiculturalism and Ethnic Attitudes in Canada*. Ministry of Supply and Services, Ottawa, 1977, p. 88.
2. Stephen Lewis Report, June 1992, p. 2. (Appendix 2 in this volume.)
3. See, for example, the federal government document *Equality Now!* Report of the Special Committee of Visible Minorities in Canadian Society. Ministry of Supply and Services, Ottawa, March 1984.

    Multiculturalism: Building the Canadian Mosaic. Report of the Standing Committee on Multiculturalism, Ministry of Supply and Services, Ottawa, 1987.

    Clare Lewis. *Race Relations and Policing Task Force*. Report to the Hon. Joan Smith, Solicitor General, Government of Ontario, Queen's Park, Toronto, 1989.

    Several numbers of *Currents*, a periodical published by The Urban Alliance on Race Relations, Toronto.
4. Paulo Freire, *Pedagogy of the Oppressed*.
5. See also Anthony Richmond, *Caribbean Immigrants*. Ministry of Supply and Services, Ottawa, 1989, pp. 20ff.
6. The Hon. T. Silipo, Bill 21: An Act to Amend the Education Act in Respect of Education Authorities and Minister's Powers, Queen's Printers for Ontario, May 1992.
7. Stephen Lewis Report, *op cit.*, p. 23.
8. *Ibid.*, p. 21.
9. John Brooks Community Foundation, *Yes, I Can!* Positive Role Models for Minority Youth. A 20-minute video produced by Sylvia Wineland.
10. The Hon. E. Ziemba, Bill 79, Government Bill tabled in the 35th Legislature, Ontario, June 25, 1992.
11. Clare Lewis, Chair, "Race Relations and Policing Task Force." Report to the Solicitor General, Ontario, 1989, p. 33.
12. Stephen Lewis Report, *op. cit.* See excerpts of this report in Appendix 2.

APPENDICES

APPENDIX 1(a)

Immigrant Selection Factors Under the Points System, Canada, 1967

	Range of points of assessment
Independent applicants	
Short-term factors	
Arranged employment or designated occupation	0 or 10
Knowledge of English and/or French	0-10
Relative in Canada	0, 3 or 5
Area of destination	0-5
Long-term factors	
Education and training	0-20
Personal qualities	0-15
Occupational demand	0-15
Occupational skill	1-10
Age	0-10
Potential maximum	100
Nominated relatives	
Long-term factors (same as for independent applicants)	1-70
Short-term settlement arrangements provided by relative in Canada	15, 20, 25 or 30
Potential maximum	100
Sponsored dependants	
Close relative in Canada willing to take responsibility for care and maintenance	Not required

To qualify for selection, independent applicants and nominated relatives normally had to earn 50 or more of the potential 100 points of assessment. In addition, they had to have received at least one point for the occupational-demand factor, to have arranged for employment or to have a designated occupation. In unusual cases, selection officers could accept or reject an independent applicant or nominated relative, regardless of the actual number of points awarded. Entrepreneurs were assessed in the same way as independent immigrants.

Source: Immigration Act, Office Consolidation (Ottawa: Supply and Services Canada, November, 1989)

APPENDIX 1(b)

Selection Criteria for Assisted Relatives and Other Independent Immigrants, Immigration Act, as Amended in 1985

		Maximum numbers of points	Remarks
1.	Education	12	One point for each year of primary and secondary education completed
2.	Specific vocational preparation	15	
3.	Experience	8	
4.	Occupational demand	15	
5.	Arranged employment or designated occupation	10	
6.	Location	5	If person intends to proceed to an area designated by the minister
7.	Age	10	10 units if aged between 18 and 35; one unit deducted for each year over 35 years
8.	Knowledge of English or French	10	10 units if fluently bilingual; 5 units if fluent in either English or French
9.	Personal suitability	10	
10.	Bonus for family class or assisted relatives	5	
	Total	100	

Under this point selection system, certain processing priorities and selection criteria apply. As described in the text, family members and refugees are admitted without having to qualify under the system, but independents and other applicants need to qualify.

The *selection criteria* according to which a visa officer assesses the immigration applications of independents and others are as follows: i) all factors of the point selection system shown above apply unless the applicant falls under categories 2 to 5 under "order of priority" below; ii) the same system applies for a would-be self-employed immigrant, except for factor 5; iii) the same system also applies for a would-be entrepreneur, except for factors 4 and 5; iv) the same system also applies for a relative-assisted immigrant applicant, except for factors 5, 6, 8 and 10; and v) in case of a retired person, the assessment is made on the basis of the intended place of residence, the presence of friends and relatives, and the immigrant's potential for adjusting to life in Canada and to support himself/herself without social benefits from provincial or federal governments. (Immigration Act, November 1989, pp. 5, 9, and 10)

The *order of priority* for processing immigrant applications is as follows: 1) members of the family class, Convention refugees, and certain designated classes of persons; 2) entrepreneurs; 3) qualified persons willing to work in a designated occupation; 4) persons with pre-arranged employment; 5) retired or self-employed persons; 6) persons who are awarded more than 8 points under occupational demand; 7) persons awarded from 4 to 8 points under occupational demand; and 8) all other immigrant applicants.

Certain changes to the selection system were introduced in the minister's annual report for 1990. These had not yet resulted in amendments to the Act or in regulatory changes at the time of writing, however.

Among those changes affecting *family immigration* were the following:

i)   In view of the inadequacy of the current definition of the concept of "close" family, the regulation for "family immigration" is changed to include, in addition to spouses and fiancé(e)s, all dependent children, all parents and dependent adopted children;

ii)   All parents of permanent residents and Canadian citizens become eligible for sponsorship as family members;

iii)   To minimize the abuse of the program by "adoptions of convenience," an independent assessment of the adoption process is required.

To improve the selection of *skilled workers*, applicants with skills required to fill national or regional occupational shortages receive an extra 10 points. About 20 to 30 percent of selected workers could be chosen from this designated occupational category. With few exceptions, all other occupations are "open," so that more emphasis is placed on education and language skills, as they are deemed to be important for the integration of immigrants into the labour market.

To prevent the build-up of *backlogs*—once there are enough immigrant applicants to meet the objectives of the immigration plan—all occupations are restricted until the existing case load is cleared.

Source: Immigration Act, Office Consolidation (Ottawa: Supply and Services Canada, November 1989).

APPENDIX 2
EXCERPTS FROM THE STEPHEN LEWIS
REPORT, JUNE 1992

The relatively brief Stephen Lewis Report in response to the Yonge Street uprising of May 1992 was released to the public on June 9, 1992. The report was rendered in eight parts, each dealing with a different but related aspect of institutional racism in the province. The issue areas are as follows:

Part 1: The Criminal Justice System
    (a) The Race Relations and Policing Task Force
    (b) A Race Relations Audit for Police Forces
    (c) Police Complaints Commissioner
    (d) The Special Investigations Unit
    (e) Use of Force
    (f) Training
    (g) An Inquiry or Review
  Part 2: Employment Equity
  Part 3: Education
  Part 4: Access to Trades and Professions
  Part 5: Ontario Training Adjustment Board
  Part 6: Ontario Anti-Racism Secretariat
  Part 7: Cabinet Committee on Race Relations
  Part 8: Community Development.

Mr. Lewis observed that what was at the bottom of the uprising was "anti-Black racism." He concluded that "just as the soothing balm of 'multiculturalism' cannot mask racism, so racism cannot mask its primary target."

Twenty-two recommendations requiring partnership action between government and the community were presented and each was accompanied with a time-table for implementation. A listing of these recommendations and a brief statement as to progress made at the time of going to press follows:

The Race Relations and Policing Task Force.
    "By July 15, 1992, the Race Relations and Policing
    Task Force be reconstituted in the person of Clare

Lewis, and any two of his former Task Force members whom he may choose. Their job will be to assess the status of current implementation, the status of recommendations still outstanding, and to suggest precisely how to proceed. Mr. Lewis should be asked to report by October 15, 1992. He should also be at liberty to make further recommendations as appropriate."

A Race Relations Audit for Police Forces.

"By September 1, 1992, a community-based Monitoring and Audit Board be established to work in conjunction with the Race Relations and Policing Unit in the Ministry of the Solicitor General. In collaboration with police forces and municipalities, a systematic audit of police race relations policies be pursued to the extent and in the number that appears reasonable in any given year."

Police Complaints Commissioner.

"By October 1, 1992, amendments to the Police Services Act be introduced to transfer the initial investigations into complaints of racially discriminatory conduct from the public complaints bureau of a police force to the Police Complaints Commissioner, and require the Police Complaints Commissioner to review the disposition by the chief of police of all such cases."

The Special Investigations Unit.

"By October 1, 1992, the Special Investigations Unit should be removed from the aegis of the Ministry of the Solicitor General, and be re-fashioned as an arms-length agency reporting to the Attorney General. It must have adequate funding to ensure a totally independent investigative capacity, and the achievement of that capacity should be the focus of its work in the immediate future."

Use of Force.

"By September 1, 1992, the Ontario Government complete the public consultation process, and have definitely in place its amendment to the Police Services Act Regulations regarding the use of force."

Training.

"By November 1, 1992, the Government of Ontario establish an Ontario Police Training, Education and Development Board with broad police and community representation, whose responsibility it would be to implement the recommendations of the Strategic Planning Committee on Police Training and Education. As a matter of urgency those recommendations which focus on race relations should be given priority."

An Inquiry or Review.

"By September 1, 1992, there be established an Inquiry into race relations and the criminal justice system, with broad terms of reference, incorporating Crown Attorneys, Courts Administration, the Judiciary, Adult and Youth correctional facilities, Community Policing, probational and parole services and all relevant particulars which the government considers germane.

By January 1, 1993, an interim report should be tabled which deals exclusively with Correctional facilities. The final report will be due July 1, 1993."

Employment Equity.

"The Employment Equity legislation should be introduced for first reading before the end of June, and if the session is for some reason prolonged, second reading should proceed. Whatever the time-table for early readings and committee consideration, the Bill should be passed by December 31, 1992, to take effect as early as possible in 1993. Furthermore, the most senior levels of the OPS should be mobilized to ensure rigorous implementation."

Education.

"The Minister of Education, through his new Assistant Deputy Minister, establish a strong monitoring mechanism to follow up the implementation of multicultural and anti-racism policies in the School Boards of Ontario.

The Minister of Education must monitor the implementation of Employment Equity in the schools of Ontario, as closely as he monitors its implementation in his own Ministry.

The Parliamentary Assistant to the Premier, Ms Zanana Akande, continue to pursue, with unrelenting tenacity, the revision of curriculum at every level of education, so that it fully reflects the profound multicultural changes in Ontario society. She might also pursue as a logical accompanying reform vital to minority students, the elimination of streaming in the school system.

The Minister of Education begin a series of urgent round-table meetings with principals' associations, area superintendents and community groups. Both school and Board officials should account to community groups for their anti-racism and multicultural curricula, and co-operate with them, school by school, in immediate implementation.

The Minister of Education must work with School Boards to ensure that the level of support for ESL and FSL programs is not permitted to decline in the face of growing needs.

The Minister of Education, in conjunction with the Minister of Colleges and Universities, review admission requirements to the Faculties of Education in Ontario, in order to make sure that the Faculties make every effort to attract and enrol qualified visible minority candidates. To this end, the proposals of the Teacher Education Council, Ontario should be given serious consideration.

The Minister of Colleges and Universities examine carefully the representative nature of Boards which govern both Colleges and Universities so that they reflect the changed society of Ontario.

The Minister of Colleges and Universities determine that Employment Equity be incorporated into the policy of every institution for which he is responsible.

The Minister of Colleges and Universities give serious consideration to the harassment and discrimination policy proposed by the Council of Regents of the Community College system, with a view to using it, with whatever appropriate amendment, as a model for post-secondary institutions."

Access to Trades and Professions.

"By October 1, 1992, the Ministry of Citizenship be directed to expand its commitment to developing a system which allows foreign trained professionals and tradespersons to work in their respective fields in Ontario. In the interim, the Ministry should draw together representatives from those who have made previous submissions on this subject, and co-operatively plan the process. Additional resources will have to be made available."

The Ontario Training and Adjustment Board.

"The Minister ensure that the labour market partners, so-called, fully reflect equity representation on the OTAB Board, and that once OTAB comes firmly on stream, the Minister insist that visible minority representation and participation in training policies and programs be given the highest priority."

The Ontario Anti-Racism Secretariat.

"By November 1, 1992, legislation be introduced to convert the Ontario Anti-Racism Secretariat into an enhanced Ontario Anti-Racism Directorate reporting directly to the Minister of Citizenship. The months between now and then should be used in the elaboration of policy, in the hiring of staff to fill current vacancies, and in the early collaboration with community groups for whom the Secretariat will be a working partner. Any new financial requirements should be provided by the end of 1992."

Cabinet Committee on Race Relations.

"By August 1, 1992, a Cabinet Committee on Race Relations be formed, to be chaired by the Minister of Citizenship, with a core of requisite Ministers. The composition of the Committee would accommodate the issues to be addressed. The Committee would meet four times a year with a Consultative Group representative of the visible minority communities. The proposed enhanced Anti-Racism Directorate would act as a secretariat to the meetings, and provide research and consultative back-up to the preparations for the meetings. The agenda would be established by or negotiated with the Consultative Group."

Community Development.
> "That the proposed Anti-Racism Directorate be asked to work with representative minority constituencies, to fashion an unprecedented community development plan which incorporates the many proposals and ideas that never seem to be examined by others."

COMMENT

These recommendations of the Stephen Lewis Report are a complex agenda requiring many new steps in very sensitive areas of race relations policy and practice—the criminal justice system, the workplace and education institutions, to name just a few. The overall process demanded extensive consultation with communities across Ontario, then initiating and concluding legislation. Besides, most of Mr. Lewis' recommendations were tied into very tight time schedules.

Thus, as we go to press, some 14 months after its release, not much that is concrete can be said to have been accomplished by the Report. There has been much talk but not sufficient positive action. A careful study of the record might very well show that while government has attempted to push its anti-racism agenda, it has been unable to control the rate at which a somewhat reluctant bureaucracy has been prepared to move to embrace change.

Note: For a fuller progress report on the recommendations, see "The Stephen Lewis Report: Current Status of Recommendations." Ministry of Citizenship Update, April 30, 1993.

APPENDIX 3
SUBMISSION TO THE
STEPHEN LEWIS INQUIRY, MAY 1992

AN INITIATIVE
To Bring About Solidarity of Purpose
Among the Various Sections of
the Black Diaspora in
Metropolitan Toronto

The objective function of this exercise is to generate a level of collective action that can come to enjoy maximum support from the Black community in setting before the Ontario Government, at this critical juncture, a plan and a program of action. Indeed, such a plan of action as can serve to convince that community of government's seriousness in halting and redressing the ravages of anti-Black racism that has been endemic, systemic and pandemic across all sectors of life in this society.

The objective condition is that, in the wake of the Yonge Street riots, the Ontario Government has indicated its concern for the initiation of remedial action by appointing the Stephen Lewis one-man task force, and requiring him to report back with a plan within a month. It is less important for the Black community to be critical of this strategy than to make optimal use of it.

The formula for optimal use of the government's "Stephen Lewis" initiative is solidarity among the Black community. It is our inescapable duty to ourselves and to our progeny to reply in a solid voice with a plan which incorporates the crucial issues in the critical sectors of public life about which the Black community grieves. It is imperative that we agree on a common plan of action to submit to the Premier, via Mr. Lewis, if this needs be the route.

My suggestion for a model around which such a plan of action might be built is as follows:

1. Identifying the Problem.
    The root of the problem is ANTI-BLACK RACISM. It is a pattern of discriminatory behaviour, both subtle and hostile, exercised against Black

Figure 5
Some Critical Spheres of Anti-Black Discrimination

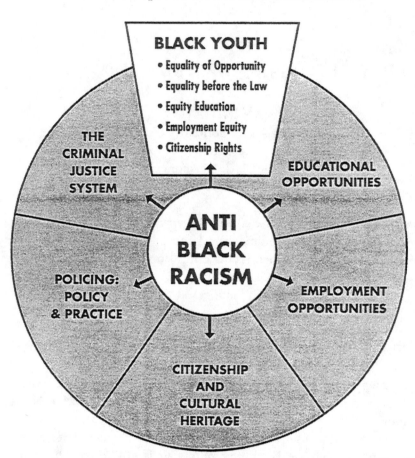

people as a distinct category within the 'visible minorities' euphemism. The discrimination is based on race and colour; it is endemic, systemic, and pandemic in its practice and influence.

2. Understanding the Dimensions of the Problem.

Anti-Black racism in inter-personal and institutional forms exhibits itself in every corner and at the very centre of this society. But it is on Black youth that the incidence falls hardest. Figure 5 illustrates this by pointing to some of the more crucial areas where racism is most brutally practised against them. And it should be the central focus of any action plan designed to correct this, that it should seek to guarantee the equality of opportunity, and to provide the leadership capabilities and coping mechanisms by which Black youth are empowered to achieve full and equal participation in all spheres of public life. The diagram emphasizes Black youth. The objective condition in which they exist is characterized by the absence of equality before the law; equality of opportunity; equity education; employment equity; and denial of heritage and citizenship rights. They are Toronto's newest under-class. And the forces which imprison them there are brutal. They include:

(i) The Criminal Justice System. In need of change are:
     Assigning of judges to cases.
     The jury selection process.
     The plea bargaining process.
     The behaviour of the trial judge in charging and directing the jury.
     The parole and rehabilitation processes.

(ii) Policing: Policy and Practice. Critical areas are:
     Public accountability—constant monitoring and evaluation.
     The use of deadly force against Blacks.
     The treatment of suspects whilst in police custody.
     The Special Investigation Unit.
     Procedures for complaints against the police.
     Race relations sensitivity training for police.
     Employment equity—time-tables and compliance.
     Community policing initiatives.

(iii) Education. The litany of insensitivities and outright malpractice is well known. Urgent measures for correction include:
     Re-wording and re-tabling of Bill 125 paying specific attention to anti-Black racist education.
     Establishing a section in the administrative functions and organizational chart of the Ministry of Education with special responsibility for the development and delivery of anti-racist and equity education.

Establishing and sustaining an Advisory Committee on anti-racist (Black) education.

Placing special emphasis on the monitoring, evaluating and inspecting of anti-racist policies and programs in school boards and schools.

Paying careful attention to teacher preparation and re-education.

Re-developing of curricula so as to allow for a central inclusion of Black ethno-specific inputs.

(iv) Employment Equity.

The pending Employment Equity Bill must be brought with renewed urgency before the House and it must contain special reference to dealing with the anti-Black racist situation.

Special attention needs to be paid to the high unemployment level among Black youth seeking their first job.

Mandatory implementation of employment equity programs should start with the Administration and the Government sector.

Enforcement and compliance procedures must be established. In particular, the media, both electronic and print, should be brought into line.

(v) Citizenship and Cultural Heritage.

As immigrants, a very low entry status is accorded Blacks. Native born Canadian Blacks are hardly ever permitted to leave this ascribed status of perpetual immigrants. The media, in particular, and all other public institutions, in general, are guilty of this blatant denial of the civic rights of Blacks. Black youth, born in Canada, feel particularly robbed of their identity and seek redress to this systematic pattern of alienation. Among the strategies for dealing with the situation are:

Community based initiatives for strengthening ethno-cultural heritages among the various sections of the Black diaspora.

The provision of support services and facilities for senior citizens, the youth and pre-schoolers in the Black community.

Figure 6
A Black Cultural Centre Project

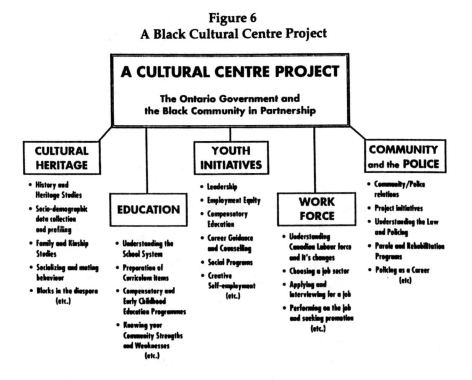

Building structures towards the development of institutional completeness within the Black community; and doing this by taking advantage of every legitimate avenue of assistance provided in the policy statements of this multi-cultural society.

3. Towards Finding Effective Solutions.

There can no longer be any doubt that the basic formula for redressing the Black condition in Canada will need to be built on the development and exercise of partnership action between all levels of government and the Black community on a continuing basis. This is especially crucial in the circumstances of Ontario and Metro Toronto. The Black community must retain the right to act alone most of the time in its own interest. The initiative will always remain its own. But the critical support of all levels of government, in terms of funding and otherwise, is an essential ingredient of the partnership. And a structure for delivery is necessary. Some recommendations for action are as follows:

(i) The establishment, in principle and in practice, of effective working partnerships between the Black community and the Ontario and municipal levels of government.

(ii) Identifiable elements of this partnership need to include Black Advisory/Consultative Committees to work on a regular, systematic basis with respective government ministries, e.g., Education, Citizenship.

(iii) The Ontario and other levels of government and their agencies must continue to provide, but on a more reliable and systematic basis, funds for projects of value to organizations within the Black community. The community should decide what is of value, and should be responsible for evaluating the effectiveness of projects on which community groups have worked.

(iv) As it has done for so many other ethno-cultural groups, the Ontario government must undertake to provide funding assistance for the acquisition of a Black-Canadian Heritage and Cultural Centre. This must be an item of high priority on the agenda for the immediate future.

(v) This Centre will provide a symbol of pride for the Black presence in Ontario and Metro. It will help foster solidarity whilst transcending diasporic differences. It will promote an image of readiness to work for the full empowerment of our young people in multi-racial, multi-ethnic, multi-lingual Ontario.

(vi) In terms of practical utility, the Centre will provide a home for networking, planning, programming and co-ordinating activities and projects of various types through which the community's multi-faceted needs and interests can flow and be met.

(vii) The partnership of Community and Government should negotiate a plan to be programmed and phased, in the first instance, over the next three years.

(viii) The management responsibilities of the Centre are, of course, to be met by the Community.

(ix)   Figure 6 presents an example of the scope of networking and programming to be headquartered in the Centre.

(x)   The long era of futile 'talking' should now be put to rest. Meaningful action, in the eyes of our young people in particular, means mobilizing and negotiating an action plan to be set in train, NOW.

W.W. (Percy) Anderson
Professor
Social Science
York University

Submission to Stephen Lewis Committee on Race Relations